Access by Design

A Guide to Universal Usability *for* Web Designers

SARAH HORTON

New Riders

ACCESS BY DESIGN: A Guide to Universal Usability for Web Designers
SARAH HORTON

New Riders
1249 Eighth Street
Berkeley, CA 94710
510 524-2178
800 283-9444
510 524-2221 (fax)
www.peachpit.com
To report errors errata@peachpit.com

Copyright © 2006 by Sarah Horton
Developmental Editor Karen Gocsik
Production Editor Hilal Sala
Copyeditor Doug Adrianson
Technical Editor Glenn Fleishman
Indexer FireCrystal Communications
Cover design Mimi Heft
Interior design Sarah Horton

New Riders is an imprint of Peachpit, a division of Pearson Education

ISBN 0-321-31140-X
9 8 7 6 5 4 3 2 1

Printed and bound in the United States of America

For my brother, Matt,
who always pushed me to reach
for the higher branch

Contents

Foreword

THE FIRST PHOTOGRAPHERS had to design and build their own cameras. As photography caught on, the needs of professional photographers stimulated camera design innovations. Fifty years passed before George Eastman designed the Kodak camera for a much wider community of users. It took another century for camera designers to include high-tech universal usability features such as automatic aperture settings and autofocus. These features enabled most users to produce quality images reliably. This story has an amazingly successful outcome: cameras are used in 96% of American households today. And now, as digital cameras and cell phones with cameras have become popular, photos will become even more ubiquitous.

Similarly, the first Web site builders had to design their own programming tools. And as Web popularity soared, the needs of Web designers influenced the software tools. With 70% of American households now using the Web for health, travel, and shopping, it is clear that the transformation to public use of the Web is here. However, user experiences are often filled with frustration aggravated by confusing layouts and failure to find what they want. Improving the quality of Web experiences and broadening the audience is the next challenge for high-technology researchers and entrepreneurs.

Fortunately, Sarah Horton's book can accelerate the pace of Web site design improvement. With clarity and thoughtful authority, Sarah lays out the territory of good design, as inspired by universal usability. Her goal is to make Web sites accessible for everyone. By this she means to improve the Web experience for all users, including those who have physical disabilities and other limitations. She assumes knowledge of HTML, CSS, and other technical issues, so she can concentrate on design. Her analysis is sophisticated but her advice is clear and easily applicable.

The chapters provide lucid examples of good and bad design for structure, text, images, tables, and forms. She guides designers through the presentation issues of links, color, audio, video, and interactivity with comprehensible guidelines and wise advice. Each guideline is nicely summarized in a section called *In a nutshell*. The advice guides designers to make sensible decisions that will benefit most users—by improving layouts, appropriately integrating images, and clarifying content. The family values of good design produce many happy children.

Sarah's book is among a growing set of efforts to improve Web design for all users. These strategies benefit users with visual, auditory, or mobility limitations and also bring gifts to older adults, users with cognitive limitations, users with low literacy, novice users, and others with particular needs. The good news is that these same strategies also benefit all users.

There is also good news from research and development workers who are increasingly mindful of clearly defined personas and audience segments. Refined evaluation methods, automated software evaluation of designs, and logging tools are providing the richer feedback needed to further improve designs. Controlled studies with selected user groups, observations of diverse users, and torrents of usage data give Web designers the evidence they need to make rational decisions for a wider range of users. As a computing professional this is satisfying to see, as I believe we will be remembered, in part, by how ambitiously we work to ensure that every Web user can successfully accomplish his or her goals.

Professionals like Sarah Horton, who address their social responsibilities to ensure broad access, are receiving recognition for their efforts. During 2005, the Association for Computing Machinery's (ACM) Special Interest Group on Computer Human Interaction (SIGCHI) established an award for social impact. The first recipient of this award was Gregg Vanderheiden of the University of Wisconsin's Trace Center.

Dr. Vanderheiden received the award for "his technical innovations and inspiring leadership in making information and communications technologies usable by more people. His contributions are especially beneficial to users with disabilities, but the techniques he developed will bring benefits to all users." He cochaired the Web Content Accessibility Guidelines Working Group, whose recommendations have had widespread international influence.

Conferences that address accessible designs are gaining strength. The ACM's Special Interest Group on Accessible Computing is actively promoting research with its Assets conferences on computers and accessibility. I am proud of organizing the ACM's Conference on Universal Usability, which generated a capacity crowd of researchers and industry leaders. The SIGCHI group has an extensive Web site devoted to accessibility as well.

In Europe, the newly formed Accessible Design in the Digital World Conference (www.accessinthedigitalworld.org) is led by the diligent and persistent efforts of Alan Newell. The event adds to the interest generated by the series of successful conferences on User Interfaces for All (UI4ALL) (http://ui4all.ics.forth.gr/) invigorated by the enthusiasm of Constantine Stephanidis, who also founded the journal, *Universal Access in the Information Society*.

Visionary leaders recognize the importance of broad participation by attending to the needs of diverse people. Thomas Jefferson wrote: "I feel... an ardent desire to see knowledge so disseminated through the mass of mankind that it may... reach even the extremes of society: beggars and kings." Similarly, two centuries later, World Wide Web creator Tim Berners-Lee emphasized the many dimensions of universality in his Japan Prize lecture: "The most important thing about the World Wide Web is that it is universal. By exploring this idea along its many axes we find a framework for considering its history, its role today, and guidance for future developments." He amplifies this idea to suggest a torrent of further innovations. Universality is a generative theme; it forces new requirements that lead to surprising benefits for many users.

The first wave of Web dissemination is spreading across the world as users learn about the possibilities and get connected. But fewer than one in six people in the world are Web users, so there will still be much turbulence as the first wave of information access rolls through. There remains much work to be done by designers in providing useful, usable, and universal content. Cross-cultural, multilingual, and multicultural designs are no longer just fashionably innovative; they are becoming required and expected. Serious attention to privacy and security is shifting from nice-to-have to need-to-have.

When 80% of humanity has access to information and is getting email, we'll need to celebrate with trumpets and fireworks. Of course, the second wave—in which users can create Web pages, produce content, and disseminate their ideas, music, photos, and products—has already begun rolling out among early-adopting users. The shift from information access to content generation is profound. eBay, wikis, and blogs are part of the second wave, which already claims several hundred million users—and that is just the beginning. The creative aspects of the second wave are enabling artists to produce animated and interactive visual and musical art projects while enabling scientists to collaborate in exploring the human genome or fighting HIV/AIDS. Open-source creativity is a potent force, especially when harnessed by the vision of universal usability. Online communities and social computing are spreading, enabling fruitful cooperation and democratic participation.

Universal usability will do more than stimulate entertainment, encourage conversation, and facilitate photo sharing. It has the potential to improve health care, enliven education, and accelerate economic development. Realizing these potentials is the goal for those who want to be heroes of the second wave.

But before we let this utopian optimism wash away our rational side, we should remember that there are serious risks. Good intentions are a fine starting point, but attention to real dangers is essential for happier outcomes. Universal usability in design is important, but economic, educational, and policy support to reduce digital divides are necessary as well. Public discussion about privacy protection, community values, and appropriate regulation can help reduce the dangers. Unfortunately, we will also need capable enforcement to cope with the spammers, spyware distributors, and stalkers. We'll need to address the deceptive advertisers and malicious identify thieves, and we'll need to develop protections from racist or terrorist groups who seek to use the universality of the Web for harmful purposes.

And what about the third wave? Can we envision ways in which Web technologies will promote effective international development, hasten innovative education, and ensure safe neighborhoods? How can we use the Web to improve health care, accelerate environmental protection, and support conflict resolution? The key to the third wave will be the transformation from information to action. A Web page on world hunger is a good start, but it does not in itself solve the problem. Information without action is failure. Knowledge without responsibility is tragic.

It is difficult to envision the impacts of our efforts, but I have come to believe that open discussion and broad participation have profound benefits. Thomas Jefferson and Tim Berners-Lee had the right idea. Open systems enable a wider range of ideas that contributes to more successful solutions. Engaging more voices not only widens the range of policy options, but it also builds commitment to the community's decision and encourages refinements as the inevitable implementation problems emerge.

Mindless optimism is dangerous because it allows darker forces to emerge, but visionary thinking is needed to create new possibilities. A mature approach balances the enthusiastic and sober sides of our personalities. Each designer makes a contribution by creating new opportunities; each designer shares responsibility for the world he or she creates. There's much work to be done. Sarah Horton has done her job well. Now it is our turn. Let's get to work!

Ben Shneiderman
University of Maryland

WE BEAR IN MIND that the object being worked on is going to be ridden in, sat upon, looked at, talked into, activated, operated, or in some other way used by people individually or en masse.

When the point of contact between the product and the people becomes a point of friction, then the… designer has failed.

On the other hand if people are made safer, more comfortable, more eager to purchase, more efficient—or just plain happier— by contact with the product, then the designer has succeeded.

HENRY DREYFUSS, *Designing for People*, 1955

Preface

THE WEB HAS DEMOCRATIZED DESIGN—both the process of design and the attendant responsibilities. Knowingly or not, we have been engaging in design throughout our lives, but without such broad implications. When we choose whether to wear brown shoes or black, the effect of our choice is limited to the people we encounter throughout the day. When we design a Web site, we design for everyone. Our choices affect anyone who tries to use our site.

Making decisions—that is the task of the designer. Good decisions have a basis: a purpose to uphold and best practices for achieving that purpose. For example, the purpose of type is to be read, and best practices provide conventions for setting type size for optimal readability. The purpose of a light switch is to control illumination, and best practices dictate how to design a light switch for optimal usability.

The purpose of a Web site is… well… that depends. The Web is dynamic and its purpose evolves as the technology grows and changes. Defining purpose depends on whether we are talking about functionality—what makes the Web work; interface—how users interact with the Web; or content—what users do with the Web. Defining *best practices* depends greatly on how we define our users—are we talking about "typical" users, cell phone users, blind users, adult users, Google?

Given the complexity of the tool, its dynamic nature, and the diversity of its users, what do we use as a basis for making design decisions when designing Web sites? This book will attempt to answer that question, and will provide guidelines for making design decisions that work for the greatest number of users.

THE ORIGINS OF THIS BOOK

I've been doing print and interface design since the beginning of my professional career and without the benefit of a design education, I have relied on the knowledge of experts to guide me: Robert Bringhurst, Patrick Lynch, Donald Norman, Ben Shneiderman, and Edward Tufte, just to name a few. This approach has served reasonably well in areas where design is established, such as graphic and interface design. However, Web design was just new when I began designing Web sites, and I had no seasoned experts to turn to for guidance in that arena. Instead, I muddled along, trying to make sense of the medium and develop an appropriate design approach. These approaches and methods have passed through several phases leading up to the methods I employ today and that I advocate in this book.

Graphic design

In the early days of the Web, when users were "surfers" skimming along the surface of the Web, Web design was about looking good. Designers went to great lengths to design sites that were eye-catching and that incorporated established design methods. Unfortunately, the medium provided few tools for graphic design, which meant a large part of my efforts went to devising methods for controlling design and layout.

Information design

Once users became more goal-oriented, information design gained importance. Too often, Web users could not find what they were looking for. In response, designers began to pay more attention to the information structure of their sites. Information architecture became part of my practice, with a focus on solid organization, clear and effective navigation, and self-explanatory labels. I started developing content inventories and site diagrams to build sound site structure, and employed user research methods, such as card sorting and user testing, to design intuitive navigation.

User-centered design (a.k.a usability or user experience)

A major paradigm shift occurred with the introduction of "users" into the Web design process. Designers began consulting users early and often for insights that would inform the decision-making process. Until this time, I felt my role as a designer was to make decisions about the design of my pages on behalf of the user, based on what I knew about graphic, interface, and information design. Once I started working with users, I found I could derive design decisions by observing user behavior and feedback. At this point, user research and usability testing began to inform many of my design decisions.

Web accessibility

When the Web community began discussing Web access for people with disabilities, some of the fundamental attributes of Web pages came into focus—attributes that had been either neglected or suppressed because they interfered with visual design. The most basic of these is flexibility—Web pages adapt to the needs and preferences of users. In understanding the breadth of diversity among Web users, I came to appreciate that flexibility was a good thing rather than something to be overcome. I stopped trying to impose design and began optimizing my pages for graceful transformation.

Web standards

About the same time, and perhaps not coincidentally, the Web design community began demanding support for Web standards. In order to design consistent pages in an inconsistent environment, Web designers had adopted complex and sometimes unorthodox methods for implementing designs that would render consistently across browsers with poor support for standards. These methods often worked at cross-purposes with accessibility and universal access—for example, favoring images over text because image-based designs provided a measure of consistency. The call for Web standards brought about better browser support for good coding practices.

By focusing on Web accessibility and Web standards, I gained a better understanding of the purpose and fundamental character of Web sites. Rather than work at odds, I started to work *with* the constructs, and the constraints, of the medium.

Universal design

In the physical world, access is often achieved using a *universal design* approach, where accessibility features are integrated into a design. Common examples include curb cuts, access ramps, and elevators. But universal design principles can be applied to appliances, devices, Web sites, even instruction—such as education programs designed to work for all kinds of learners. The basic premise behind universal design is to provide for diversity through design rather than accommodation—for example, rather than providing handicapped access via a separate entry, one would integrate ramped access into the main entrance.

As a Web designer concerned with accessibility, I was attracted to the concept of providing a single point of access that would work for all users. I liked the idea of incorporating access requirements into my designs rather than considering them as an afterthought. By adopting a universal design approach, I could make access a deliberate part of my Web design process. I would address access requirements within the overall design of a Web page with the goal of optimizing page designs to work for all users. *Access by design* became my *modus operandi*.

However, the term *universal design* conjures images from the physical world, such as access ramps, curb cuts, and kitchen gadgets, more so than Web pages. So while I adopted a universal design approach, I had difficulty advocating the method because the term *universal design* has not found its way into the general discourse of Web design.

Universal usability

I was well into writing this book when I discovered that Ben Shneiderman was advocating a design concept that addressed universal design specifically for communications and information technologies. Shneiderman has long been a leader in user-centered interface design. His seminal book, *Designing the User Interface*, first published in 1986, is required reading for fledgling computer scientists worldwide. He has been one of the most prominent advocates of the "human" in human-computer interaction.

In his most recent book, *Leonardo's Laptop*, Shneiderman defines *universal usability* as "enabling all citizens to succeed using communication and information technology in their tasks." For Shneiderman, citizens include users with "new or old computers, fast or slow network connections, and small or large screens, … young and old, novice and expert, able and disabled, … those yearning for literacy, overcoming insecurities, and coping with varied limitations." This broad and encompassing view of the user resonated with my universal design approach. I felt the Web could support this type of universality. I also liked his focus on usability over accessibility. As an interface designer, Shneiderman understands that access to content and functions is the basis of universality, but that access alone is not enough. Many Web sites that meet the standards and guidelines for accessibility are not usable. Having found a way to describe the design approach I had been seeking, I adopted the label *universal usability* as both a design methodology and the focus for this book.

THE FOCUS OF THIS BOOK
To achieve universal usability, Shneiderman identifies three challenges for designers: "to support a wide range of technologies, to accommodate diverse users, and to help users bridge the gap between what they know and what they need to know." In order to apply these general challenges specifically to Web design, we need to consider the layers of Web site design: function, interface, and content.

♦   Function: The things we design take their form from their functions. A coffee mug must have the right shape, capacity, and material to contain and dispense hot liquid. Part of designing for function is identifying the restrictions inherent in whatever we are designing: A coffee mug cannot leak and must be well insulated so the user does not get burned. On the Web, the functional layer consists of the technical underpinnings that make a Web site work. When a Web site is functional, its content is accessible and its interactive components function properly.

♦ Interface: Well-designed objects are self-explanatory. One look at a coffee mug and we know it's for holding and drinking liquid. We know how to work it by the way it's shaped: The hollow is for filling, the lip is for drinking, the handle is for grasping. Having access to a Web site and its functions does not necessarily make it usable. A usable Web site tells the user what it's for and how it works. It offers an interface that clearly conveys purpose and provides self-explanatory controls.

♦ Content: If function and interface are the means, then content is the end. In many areas of design, the designer is not responsible for content. For example, it is the user who decides what kind of coffee goes inside the coffee mug. In the Web domain, content can be countless different things—information, entertainment, a conversation, a transaction. A Web designer *is* responsible for what goes in the cup, and whether it's instant or brewed is reflected on the design of the site.

In this book, we primarily address universal usability at the *functional* layer, focusing on the challenges of designing pages that are accessible and usable on different devices by diverse users. We concentrate on the functional layer because, without it, the other layers are irrelevant. An intuitive interface and informative content are useless if the basic functions of a site don't work. Like a car that doesn't start, a Web site that does not function is of no value to the user.

CONVENTIONS AND TERMS USED IN THIS BOOK

This book is organized around best-practice guidelines for universal usability. It begins with an introduction that lays the foundation for universal usability, and the remainder of the book is divided into chapters that address concerns as they relate to different elements of Web pages.

Each chapter begins with an overview and is followed by guidelines. The guidelines are broken into sections: first, basic principles covering the broad concerns associated with the element, and then more specific concerns relating to particular aspects of the element, such as markup, size, and color. Each guideline is summarized in a section marked "In a nutshell." Sections and guidelines are numbered for orientation and easy reference, and the Appendix contains a quick reference to all the guidelines and nutshells.

Before we begin, let's take a moment to define the terms used in this book.

Design

Design is a problematic label to assign to the process of making Web sites. The term feels too big—too much an assessment of worth. We think that things that are "designed" must look good. But design is, simply, the process of making decisions about how things are made—their size, shape, materials, and so on. There are many design fields—engineering, graphic design, industrial design, architecture—and many things created—safety pins, billboards, armchairs, towns. Although we often think of design purely in terms of its aesthetic aspects, design is what gives form to *all* aspects of our creations. Whenever we make a choice about how a thing is made—how it looks, how it operates, how it is put together—we are engaging in the process of design.

In this book, when we talk about design we are talking about the process of making the decisions that give form to a Web site.

Designers

The term *designers* is also difficult. We think of designers as well-clad people who make decisions about the buildings that we live in, the clothing that we wear, and the devices that we use. We may not feel qualified to think of ourselves as designers. However, any time a person makes something, the process involves some degree of design. Consequently, at some point in time, we are all designers, whether of sand castles, soup, or sonograms.

In this book, when we refer to designers we are not talking *only* about people who are educated in a design discipline. Professional designers design Web sites, but so do countless other people—educators, entrepreneurs, musicians, gamers, medical professionals, shopkeepers, architects, and so on. If design is the process of making choices about how things are made, then Web designers are people who make Web sites.

Users

Another source of conflict is in defining the audience. We design for "people," and when we design well, people become "users." When we refer to "people," we are not talking about your average José and Joséfa—we mean all people. Given the diversity of human needs, it may seem unrealistic to discuss design in such broad and inclusive terms. How could all people use a single Web site? We forget that we are designing Web sites, not T-shirts, and that, on the Web, one size *can* fit all.

Some people avoid the label *users* when referring to people who use Web sites. In this book we favor the label because it emphasizes the role of the designer. We build Web sites so people can *use* them. When we make a Web site that is usable, people become "users."

SO, WE HAVE ESTABLISHED that, as makers of Web sites, we are designers engaged in the process of design. We are interested in humanizing the Web by designing Web sites that people, in all their diversity, can use. To build sites that are universally usable, we must base our designs on a framework of solid functionality. Let's begin.

Introduction

DESIGN IS A MEANS TO AN END. We design things for a purpose. We design beds to sleep in. We design clocks to keep track of time. Our success at these activities (the end) depends on the design of the tools (the means). With good design, the tool fits the task so neatly that it becomes part of the task. Instead of using a bed, we sleep. Instead of using a clock, we check the time.

We build Web sites for many reasons, but one reason trumps all others: We build Web sites so people can use them. They are to be looked at, watched, listened to, skimmed, read, printed, clicked, input into, and operated by different people using different access devices. If the result of design is that someone cannot load a page or activate a link or read a paragraph or interpret an image, then design is no longer a means to an end—design is an impediment.

A FUNCTIONAL BASIS FOR DESIGN

It wasn't by observing buildings that architect Louis H. Sullivan arrived at the formula "form follows function." It was by observing forms in nature.

> "Whether it be the sweeping eagle in his flight, or the open apple-blossom, the toiling work-horse, the blithe swan, the branching oak, the winding stream at its base, the drifting clouds, over all the coursing sun, *form ever follows function,* and this is the law. Where function does not change form does not change. The granite rocks, the ever-brooding hills, remain for ages; the lightning lives, comes into shape, and dies in a twinkling."

In his essay "The Tall Office Building Artistically Considered," Sullivan asserts that the pervading law of nature should be the law of all things, built by man or nature.

Of course, nature does not build Web sites—people do. Sullivan would ask that Web designers hold *as law* that form follows function. To follow this dictum, we must first define in plain detail what a Web site is for, and examine the functions that the Web provides. Only by defining the function of the Web can we make appropriate decisions about its form.

DEFINING FUNCTION

When thinking about function, we tend to focus on the function of the site we are designing—selling books, publishing texts, building community—rather than on the functions of the Web itself. Our decision making has more to do with information structure, visual design, and back-end technologies than with basic functionality. We might say we have this focus because our design methods ensure a working Web site. Unfortunately, basic functionality is not a given. We all have experienced Web sites that look good and are well organized but that are nonfunctional on some basic level: forms that don't submit, broken links, unreadable text. The fact is, the Web is broken at least part of the time for everyone who uses it. For people with special needs, the Web is broken much of the time. Our tendency to focus on the features of a site is part of the problem.

When we focus primarily on features, we risk making choices that impair basic functionality and lead to nonfunctional sites. To design functional sites, we must understand the purpose and functions of the Web, and the attributes that make it something that people can use.

To define function we must first identify our audience.

Who (or what) is the audience for Web pages?

In the most abstract sense, we build Web pages so that computers can read them. The software that people use to access Web pages is what "reads" the document. How the page is rendered depends on the type of software being used. A visual browser, such as Netscape or Safari, will render pages with images and complex layouts. A text-only browser, such as Lynx, will render only the text and minimal formatting. A talking browser, such as Home Page Reader, speaks the contents of a Web page. There are other types of software that read Web pages: Email harvesting programs read Web pages to extract email addresses; search-engine software reads pages to place them in a Web page catalog. When considered in the broadest sense, our primary audience is computers. Our Web pages must be usable by computers.

Of course, *people* use computers, and as we work our way from the general to the specific we are concerned with two types of users: visual and nonvisual. Visual users are those who use the Web by viewing pages on some sort of display device; nonvisual users hear them read aloud or interface with the underlying code. According to this definition, nonvisual users include software applications—such as Google.

So our most general definition of audience includes the following:

♦ Visual users: look at visually rendered Web pages.
♦ Nonvisual users: hear pages read aloud or read the underlying code.

If we sharpen our focus, we see important subdivisions within these categories: *Software that reads what?* Email addresses? Page content? Structural information? *People who look at pages on what?* Paper? A cell phone? A large display monitor? *People who hear pages read aloud why?* Because they can't see? Because they understand the content better that way? Because they are occupied, for example, driving a car?

These subcategories are important, and we will discuss them as we delve into the specifics of Web page elements. For now, in the spirit of simplicity and clarity, these broad audience categories will serve us well as we turn to defining the functionality of Web sites.

FIGURE 1

The Smith & Hawken
site is informative and
interactive—users can
learn about and purchase
products. For universal
usability, the information
must be accessible and
the interactive features
must be functional and
operable.

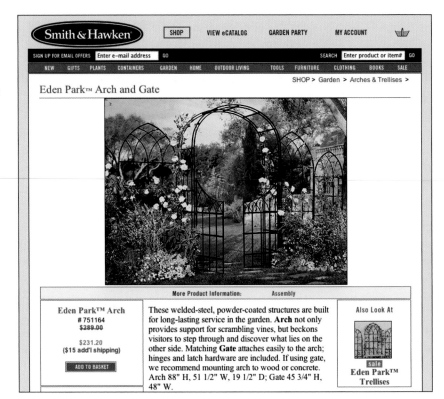

What are the functions of Web pages?

Web pages provide two basic functions: communication and interaction.

Communication: People consume information on Web pages. Some Web content is static and is meant to be ingested by the user. For example, a product page, containing a paragraph about the product and a product photo, is intended to communicate information about the product (**Figure 1**). When successful, the user ends up knowing more about the product—what it is and what it looks like.

The purpose of the description is to tell people about the product. Since the description is textual, the text must, above all, be perceivable by the user. It must be clear to the user that there is text on the page. For visual users, the text must be readable. For nonvisual users, text must be machine-friendly so it can be read well by software.

The purpose of the photo is to show people what the product looks like. For the photo to fulfill its purpose, it must be perceivable—people must know that there is a photo on the page, and that it is a photo of the product. However, the purpose of the image is to convey the visual properties of the product. To fulfill its purpose, the image must be interpretable. Visual users need to be able to view the image well enough to see its visual properties. Nonvisual users will not be able to see the image and will need the description of visual properties in a text format.

For content whose primary function is to be communicated to the user, the most important attribute is accessibility. For communication to occur, all elements must be available and accessible to the user.

Interaction: People work with Web pages. Other Web content is intended for interaction. Take, for example, a text link to a complete product description. The text of the link is both informative and functional. The link needs to be identified as a link, needs to communicate its destination, and, on activation, needs to move the user to the designated page. A functional link transports the user successfully from one page to another.

In addition to being accessible, interactive Web content must be functional. If a user does not recognize a link, cannot activate a link, or cannot reach the target page, the conditions of a link are not met.

So the basic functions of Web pages, in priority order, are

♦ Communication: Web pages communicate information. The important condition for communication is accessibility.
♦ Interaction: Web pages support user interaction. The important condition for interaction to occur is functionality.

What are the attributes of the Web?

Having defined the basic functions of the Web, we will consider the attributes that enable those functions.

Text-based: The Web is universal because it is powered by text. Text is the *lingua franca* of computer technologies because text can be read and "understood" by computers. In other words, software reads and performs actions based on text commands.

Web browser software performs certain actions based on the text it reads in Web documents. When reading text contained within a title tag, the software displays the text in the window title bar of the browser window. When reading text within the body tag, the software displays the text in the browser window. On encountering an image tag, the software retrieves the image file and displays the image in the appropriate location on the page.

With basic text, the computer can readily read and render a document. This rendering can vary depending on the environment. Browser software adapts its display to different display devices. Some browser software renders only the text in a document, ignoring visual elements and layout. Some browser software uses text-to-speech technology to read Web pages aloud. When people interact with browser software using spoken commands, the software converts spoken speech to text so the browser can respond appropriately.

When Web content is presented as text, *communication* can occur.

Structured: The Web is smart because of document structure. Software can read text but cannot attribute meaning without additional information. Document structure supplies meaning through tags that provide defining information for key document elements. Then, when reading, software can interpret certain aspects of a document. For example, if a phrase is tagged as the primary heading of an article, software can determine what the article is about.

When software has a way of deriving meaning, it can do far more than with text alone. Think about the functions of a search engine. If search engine software could only read text, a search for pages about the "tufted titmouse" would return all pages that contain those words, at best listed in order of frequency. With structured text, the software can find documents that are *about* the tufted titmouse because those words appear in the TITLE and/or H1 tag.

Standard browser software also makes use of structural codes, such as the document title. If a phrase is marked as TITLE, then software makes the assumption that the phrase identifies the document and should appear in the window title and the bookmarks list.

Software that reads Web pages aloud can communicate more information with structured text than with plain text. Many documents provide visual cues to communicate emphasis and document structure, such as italicized words and section headings. Screen reader software cannot know why a word or phrase is italicized or bold. Is it a heading? Is it emphasis? Is it a citation? Hence, these visual cues are not communicated by screen reader software. When reading a structured document, a screen reader can use audible emphasis to communicate structure to the user. Emphasis can be conveyed through a change in inflection, and document structure through sounds and inflection: for example, through a beep and slowed reading.

When Web content is structured, *meaningful communication* can occur.

Operable: The Web is interactive because it has working parts. Web pages are not merely for consumption. People operate Web pages. For the Web to be interactive, its functional parts must be in working order.

To work a Web page, we operate some sort of input device—either a pointing device like a mouse or a device that issues commands that are associated with the keyboard. Pointing devices are not usable by everyone. Some prefer to use the keyboard. Others find it difficult or impossible to work a mouse, or cannot see the screen to point and click.

On the other hand, keyboard commands can be issued using many different input devices. Commands can be input directly from the keyboard or by using spoken commands that activate keyboard actions. A variety of alternative input devices are available, and they all work by activating keyboard actions. Accordingly, all functional elements must be operable from the keyboard.

Clearly, operability is more than making sure all working parts are operable. They need to work properly and according to expectation. For instance, a link might be clickable, but if it leads to "Page not found," it cannot be considered functional. A link that is embedded in an image may be operable, but if it cannot be seen and does not include alt-text that describes the target, then people who can't see it won't know where it leads.

When Web pages are operable and function according to expectations, *interaction* can occur.

Flexible: The Web is usable because users can control their experience. In the physical world, we can't make a microwave easier to use by making the buttons larger, or shrink a book so it fits better in our handbag. Our experience of these objects is based on their design. On the other hand, some objects provide a measure of customization. As drivers, we can adjust the car seat and steering wheel to fit our size. Handbags and backpacks have adjustable straps. Since the marketplace is rife with goods, we can improve our experience by trying out different versions of the same thing. We might try several different styles of garden rakes, hiking boots, or toothbrushes, to find the one that suits us best. Or we might choose a style that has been designed to meet certain needs, such as large-print books.

When creating a fixed object, such as a book, the designer must make decisions about format—size, typeface, line length, etc. Since the aim is to create something that is usable by the largest number of people, these decisions must be based on what works best for the "average" person. In the case of a book, type size is generally set at a size that is comfortable for people with 20/20 vision.

Universal design is an approach to design that attempts to incorporate features that make things usable by more than just the "average" person. By anticipating the needs of all people, things can be designed in a way that makes them universally usable. In a public restroom, for example, the hand dryer and paper towel dispenser need to be used by standing adults, small children, and people in wheelchairs. Locating these features at a lower height makes then reachable by all.

The physical world is not an easy place to achieve universal usability. Most of what we see around us is fixed in form. For universal access and usability, one solution must address the needs of many. However, without the possibility of customization, the notion of one-size-fits-all means that someone has to compromise. For example, tall people might have difficulty using a paper towel dispenser that is located low enough for a wheelchair user. A truly universal design would adapt to meet the needs of each user.

The Web is an ideal medium for universal design. The stuff of the Web can adapt to meet the needs of each user. Much of the Web's flexibility comes from its basic structure: Web content is flexible and device-independent. Because the Web is flexible and can be customized, the user is part of the design process and can make design decisions. For instance, although the Web designer makes decisions about format, the reader has the option to display text in whatever fashion he or she chooses. Printed text is generally read off a page; Web text can be read off a page, from a screen, by software, and so on.

Flexibility is also present in the way the Web functions. We can choose to interact with the Web's operable elements (links, forms, menus, media controllers) using different methods, such as pointing and clicking, using the keyboard, touching the screen, or issuing spoken commands.

By separating content from form, the Web is also device-independent. In other words, its form is not necessarily what defines the user experience. Users can define their own experience through the devices they use to interact with the Web.

When Web pages are flexible and device-independent, *communication* and *interaction* can occur *for more users.*

PROVIDING FUNCTION

For universal usability, make Web pages text-based, structured, operable, and flexible. Although this directive sounds simple, Web sites rarely provide this most basic functionality. For example, Web sites commonly use images as links. To be functional, these links need to be accessible, which means image links need alternate text for people who can't see them. Many Web sites do not provide alternate text for images. And even with alternate text, image links do not work for visual users who need large text for reading because images cannot be resized the way text can. Moreover, image links do not adapt as well as text to different window widths, which may affect people using small devices. Clearly, image links significantly impair functionality, yet they are a common element on many sites (**Figure 2**). How can this be? *Because decisions about form often take precedence over function.*

When it comes time to make design decisions about form, particularly with a device as complex as the Web, designers must compromise. In the example above, links should not appear as images because of functional considerations. However, we sometimes use images for links to enhance the appearance of a site: for example, to use a special typeface or type treatment that we cannot achieve using plain text. We might want to enforce a certain layout that people cannot resize or alter. In these cases, form and function are in conflict. If we use images as links, we get the form we are after but we sacrifice function. Some people will not be able to access and use our pages if we use image links.

Quality Web sites that are universally usable are not simple to design and build. But building quality sites is no more difficult than designing and building Web sites that are *not* good and *not* usable. Universal design is simply an approach to design, one that requires that we make intelligent decisions that honor and uphold the function of the Web.

Making informed decisions

We cannot build a Web site without making decisions about what colors to use, what fonts to use, how to lay out pages, how to label navigation. We may make decisions based on what we think works well in our

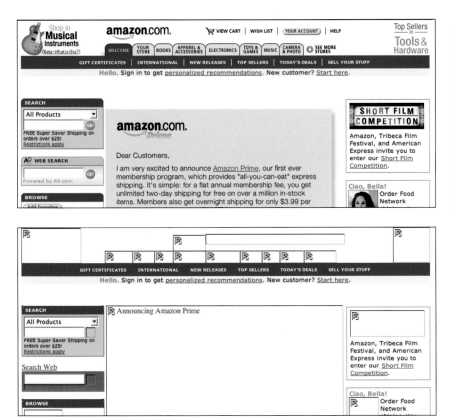

FIGURE 2

Amazon uses graphic text for links and content. Not all the graphic elements have alternate text; those that do have unhelpful alt-text. Users who cannot access image-based content and functionality may be unable to use the Amazon site.

experience of the Web. We may make decisions by emulating methods used on other sites. We may make decisions based on knowledge of best practices.

Regardless of method, somewhere along the way in the design process we will face a difficult decision, one whose effect ripples out to our other design choices. For example, we may decide to use a three-column fixed layout, even though it undermines the flexibility of our pages. When facing this type of decision, we need to determine whether the cost of a three-column layout is worth the benefit.

First, let's look at the benefits of both approaches. One benefit of a multicolumn layout is *visibility*: more content can appear "above the

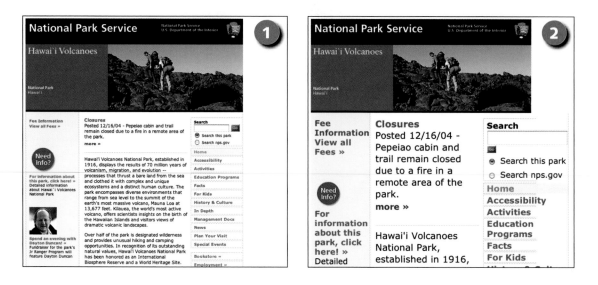

fold." Another benefit is *readability*, since fixed-width columns result in shorter lines of text. On the other hand, a flexible layout more gracefully accommodates modifications, such as enlarged type. Flexible pages also adapt to different display devices, from computer monitors to cell phones.

Now, let's look at costs. The cost of using a fixed, three-column layout is high because such a layout affects the basic accessibility and usability of a site. People who need large type for reading or who view the Web on a small device like a cell phone will either be unable to use the site or significantly hindered by the layout (**Figure 3**). The cost of *not* using a three-column fixed layout also affects usability, but in a less fundamental way. Some people might miss content if they do not scroll down to see what's below the fold. People who view Web pages on large monitors might object to long lines of text (**Figure 4**).

Now, we could make this decision based on intuition about what is important or according to personal preference. However, it is far better to make a deliberate decision that honors and upholds the basic functionality of the Web. And since we have joined hands and agreed that our primary goal for creating a Web site is so people can use it, we

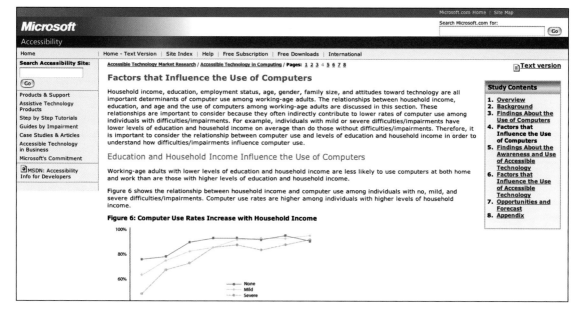

Microsoft
Accessibility

FIGURE 4

Flexible layouts, such as those on the Microsoft site, expand and collapse to fill the browser window. A flexible approach adapts well to different devices and to user modifications. However, users viewing flexible pages in a wide browser window may find the line length too long for comfortable reading.

will not compromise *flexibility* for *visibility* and *readability* because the benefit does not outweigh the cost.

Upholding the basic goals of access and usability simplifies the decision-making process significantly. Whenever the result of a design decision is that people cannot use our site, then other methods must be considered. In this case, a two-column flexible layout will meet our basic accessibility and usability goals while allowing more on-screen content and adjustable column widths.

Partnering with users

If we were to take a real-world approach to delivering a document to different users, we would provide a large-print version, an audio version, a high-contrast version, a text-only version—and still there would be people whose needs were not accommodated. In the physical world made of solid matter, it is impossible to create a thing, or even many versions of a thing, that works for everyone.

The Web provides a customizable interface to Web content. As long as the content is coded properly and designed to be flexible, users can change parameters, such as text size and color, and can use different software and devices to access Web pages. The result is that both designers and users are responsible for the design of Web pages. In a way, Web design is collaborative design. Designers send content to the user in a way that is flexible, operable, text-based, and structured; users, in turn, "redesign" the content to fit their needs and preferences.

Fixed design: Decisions based on rules and conventions. When graphic designers started working with the medium in the mid-1990s, we balked at the notion of collaboration. The rules and conventions of graphic design were established to enable effective communication. If users had the ability to change elements of a Web page, they might violate established conventions, and this was bad for communication. In response, our goal became to design pages that could *not* be customized by the user, to ensure design integrity and effective communication. We built pages with fixed elements—fixed-size text, graphic text, fixed column

FIGURE 5
User modifications are difficult to accommodate when layouts are as complex as those used on the ESPN site. This type of design relies on pixel-level precision and requires the use of graphic text and fixed-width columns to ensure the integrity of the design.

widths—that did not change size or reflow (**Figure 5**). With the advent of style sheets, we gained additional control over page elements: pixel-based sizing and positioning, leading, link formatting. Technologies such as Flash and PDF allowed us even more control over the look and feel of Web documents. Indeed, the Web gained popularity in part because it was more visually appealing than in its early, gawky days as a collection of hyperlinked text documents with scarcely any visual attributes. However, while gaining control of the user interface, we lost the active participation of the user.

In the physical world, whether we are designing razors, refrigerators, parks, or buildings, we must make decisions about how things look and how they operate. Generally, we make decisions based on a concept of what works best for the user. In user-centered design, users are consulted early and often in the design process. Established best practices are an effective source for determining what is in the best interests of the user. However, it's impossible to make design decisions that work for everyone. The way to meet the needs of a diverse population is to allow users to make their own decisions about how things look and operate.

Transitioning roles to fit the medium. When new technologies are invented, we often apply proven methods, particularly when we see the new technology as compatible with existing methods. Problems arise when this approach causes us to make inappropriate use of the new technology. While compatibility can lead us to adopt a new idea, it can also lead to misadoption if we incorrectly interpret the intended use.

Designers are accustomed to controlling design in other information and communication technologies, such as film, print, and product design. The Web is yet another communication medium, so our initial approach was to control design in the same way by applying established design conventions. This was an instance of misadoption.

The trouble with imposing established conventions on the Web is that they undermine the strengths of the medium. In the words of Tim Berners-Lee, the inventor of the Web, "The power of the Web is in its universality." When we impose a design on Web users and withhold their ability to control and customize their view, the Web becomes less universal because some people cannot use it.

For example, in order to support universal access, browsers display underlining as well as color to identify Web links. Underlining is essentially a fallback, so people who cannot distinguish color will still be able to identify links. However, underlining is considered vulgar in typographic design—a carryover from the days of the typewriter, when text styles such as italics were not readily available. There are good reasons to avoid underlines: they intersect text forms and clutter the page.

When graphic designers first started working with the Web, we objected to underlines because of their effect on legibility and readability. Asking people to read from the screen was bad enough without making them deal with underlines. However, we had little recourse since the user, not the designer, controlled the display of underlines. Though we could turn off underlining in our own browser preferences, we had to accept that our pages might or might not be displayed with links underlined. Then, with the adoption of style sheets, we gained the ability to remove link underlines, and there was much rejoicing. In today's designs, links are often displayed without underlines.

The thing is, underlines are a rather useful method for identifying links, particularly for people who cannot see color. When underlining is turned off and there is no other method for identifying links, people who cannot distinguish link color from text color cannot easily identify links. A Web site without links is like a bicycle without wheels. When we impose conventions from print typography by removing link underlines, we take away one of the most essential Web functions—hyperlinks. And while users who object to link underlines have ready browser controls to remove them, users who need link underlines cannot easily put them back.

While misadoption can end in failure, it can also lead to movement away from old ways as the potential of the new medium is realized. In the early days of film, it took some time before filmmakers stopped filming staged action in the studio and began shooting live action in different locations. In recent years, we have started to reexamine our assessment of the purpose and use of the Web.

Initially, people accessed the Web using computers and standard display monitors, which allowed designers to predict to some degree how pages would be viewed. Today, with the proliferation of access devices and different "page" dimensions, we see the futility of trying to design a single page "view" (**Figure 6**).

FIGURE 6

Flexible sites, such as the HubbleSite, are not designed with one page size in mind. Instead, the pages are designed to adapt to different dimensions.

Concerns about Web accessibility are being voiced through various channels. The Web presents opportunities for people with a great diversity of needs and preferences. Since Web content can be flexible and device-independent, the Web has great potential for people who have access or viewing requirements, use specialized software, possess old hardware and software, or have slow access to the Internet. Influential organizations like the World Wide Web Consortium are raising awareness about accessibility concerns through their Web Accessibility Initiative. Federal and local governments, organizations, and institutions are mandating Web accessibility.

All this focus on access and usability has given us the opportunity to reevaluate our role. We are accustomed to bearing responsibility for design decisions, but perhaps the Web asks something different of design. Should we continue to see ourselves as sole purveyors of design, and risk alienating users by our design decisions, or should we partner with users to build a Web that is accessible and usable by all?

Flexible design: A collaboration between design and user. Partnering with users requires two things: First, we have to design for transformation. Our pages must have flexible elements, and the overall design must hold up to change. Second, we need to recognize and respect the boundaries of the user domain.

Design for transformation means that designers must make decisions about the way Web pages are presented to the users while keeping those settings fluid so users have the ability to override settings and change elements without "breaking" the page. For example, users must be able to resize text without sending the layout into disarray. Users must be able to view pages on different display devices—large and small—and the layout must adapt gracefully. Pages must be designed using style sheets so users can override the designer settings with a custom style sheet. Pages must display well without visual formatting so users who do not use styles can still use the page (**Figure 7**). Content must be provided as text so users can suppress the display of images and still use the Web page.

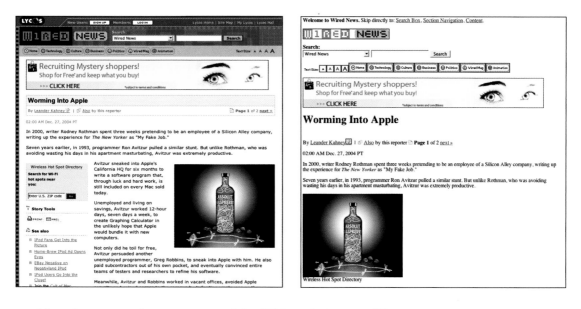

Users have control over aspects of the Web environment. They control where the cursor is on the page, what links to click on, whether to reload a page, whether to use author-defined styles or their own, how to print pages, whether links open in a new window, whether images display, and so on. Web technology gives the designer control over some of these aspects. For example, we can move the cursor focus or force a page to reload. Sometimes we do enter the user domain in order to do something helpful, like place the cursor in the search field or update a page with dynamic information, like a stock quote. However, these helpful interventions can cause considerable confusion because they violate user expectations.

For example, designers often make links to external Web sites open in a new window. We do this for good purpose. One of the problems with hypertext is that, in clicking on link after link, people can easily get lost. The back button is commonly used to return to the originating site, but it has its flaws and does not always work according to expectation. To help users return to our site, we open links in a new window so users can easily close the ancillary window and return to our site.

FIGURE 7

Wired uses style sheets to control formatting and to position elements on the page. Since content and visual design are separate, users who view the pages without styles can still access the content and functionality of the site.

FIGURE 8
Browsers offer users the
option of opening links
in a new tab or window.

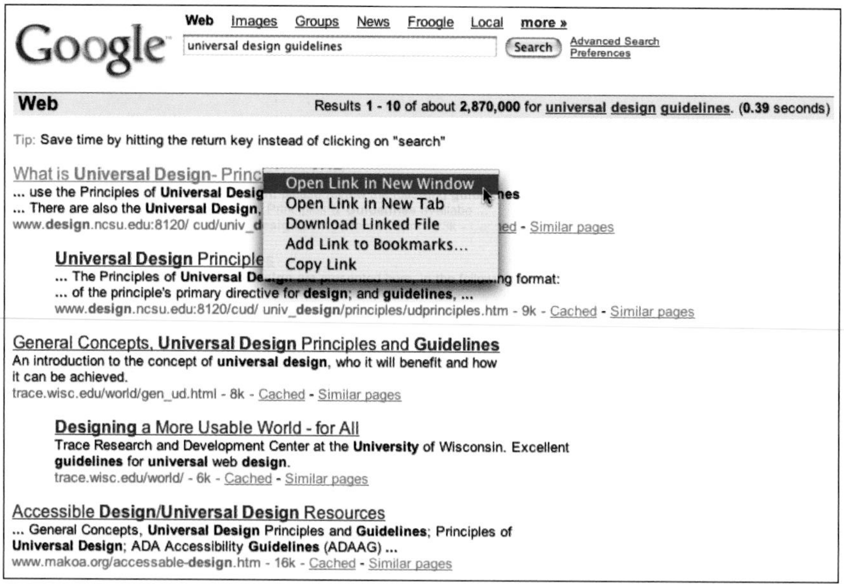

The trouble with this approach is that many Web users have a two-pronged strategy for navigating the Web. They set out by following page links, and then use the back button to retrace their steps. When a link opens in a new window, the browser establishes a new history for that window. When it comes time to head back, clicking on the back button does not work, since the originating site is not in the history for that window. A user with only those two navigation methods—following links and using the back button—is stuck and without options.

However, users have the option of opening links in a new window—this functionality is part of the user domain. Should a user find this strategy useful, she or he can easily implement this approach using built-in browser controls (**Figure 8**).

This scenario represents another instance where the user cannot override a designer's choice, but *can* implement it—an important distinction for collaborative design. If we remove link underlines so users don't have to deal with clutter, users who need underlines can't put them back. If we force links to open a new window, users who want to use the back button can't make links open in the same window. If we refresh pages to display current content, users who want a static page can't override the refresh. But users can manage all these actions—removing links, opening pages in a new window, refreshing pages—through their browser interface. When considering design choices that may cause problems for some users, we should step back and let users make their own decisions.

SUMMARY

We design Web sites so people can use them. *People* doesn't mean "some people" or "certain people." With universal usability, our goal is to design Web sites that accommodate the diversity of people and the Web browsing devices that they use. To design Web sites that people can use, we must work within the flexible framework that the Web provides.

To this end, we must begin our process with a solid understanding of how the Web works. When we know its nature, we can make intelligent design decisions that uphold rather than impede its functionality. Whenever we face a decision that may impact function, we must look for other options.

No matter how well we uphold function, we cannot possibly design a Web site that meets the needs and preferences of every user. The only reason universal usability is a realistic goal for Web sites is because the Web is a flexible medium where designers and users *share* control of its design. With a working partnership, designers provide content that is well designed but flexible, and users adapt the design as necessary. To arrive at a successful collaboration, designers must assume less control and invite users to take more responsibility for their environment.

CHAPTER 1

Fundamentals

FOR WEB SITES TO BE FUNCTIONAL, their content must be accessible and their functions operable—these are basic requirements. When we consider these requirements within the context of a universal Web, with its diversity of users and access technologies, several fundamental principles emerge to guide our efforts toward universal usability.

The most basic principle is to design simply. This applies to all areas where design is in the service of function. In *The Elements of Typographical Design*, Robert Bringhurst asserts, "Typography exists to honor content." On the Web, design exists to enable access to content and functionality. Bringhurst goes on to say, "Typography... aspires to a kind of statuesque transparency." The same holds true for Web design. A well-designed Web site has just enough emphasis to spark interest and draw attention to important elements, but not so much as to distract the user from content or to hinder functionality. In Web design, the best way to achieve a balance between engaging and overwhelming the user is to apply the simplest solution to any design problem. Simple solutions produce simple, clean pages that load quickly and are easier to maintain (**Figure 1.1**, *next page*).

From a construction standpoint, designers are well outfitted for building universally usable Web sites. The Web was designed to support universal access, and access features are integral to the technology. One method for providing universal access is using fallbacks—content presented in alternate formats to meet the needs of different users. In many cases, the provision for fallbacks is built into Web markup, such as alt-text for images.

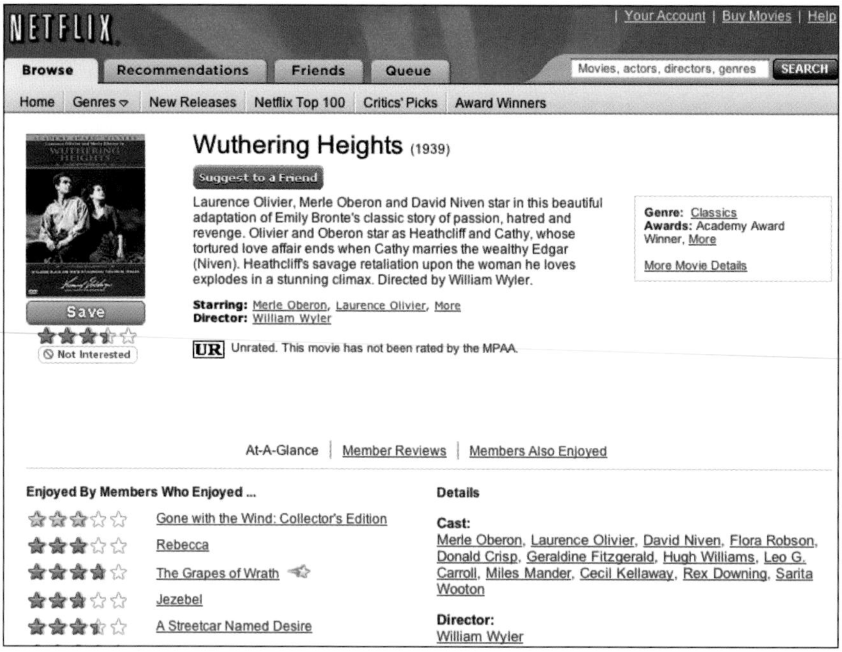

FIGURE 1.1

The Netflix site is simple, clean, and easy on the eye, with no superfluous elements demanding attention. The site features services and content rather than branding and design.

The Web can accommodate alternate formats, such as PDF, Flash, and Shockwave. In general, these formats are inferior to HTML for providing universal usability. Many alternate formats have tried to accommodate accessibility concerns by adding features such as support for structural markup and keyboard access, but these features are not integral to the format as they are with HTML. Alternate formats should be used only as an alternative to accessible HTML.

From a markup perspective, universal usability relies on three fundamental attributes: keyboard accessibility, flexibility, and user control.

Web pages have controls that users must be able to operate in order for a page to be functional. Interactive interfaces rely on user input to trigger actions. Some users do not use a pointing device, such as a mouse, but provide input either through a keyboard or some other device that activates keyboard controls. For these users, actionable items such as buttons, links, and forms must be workable using the keyboard.

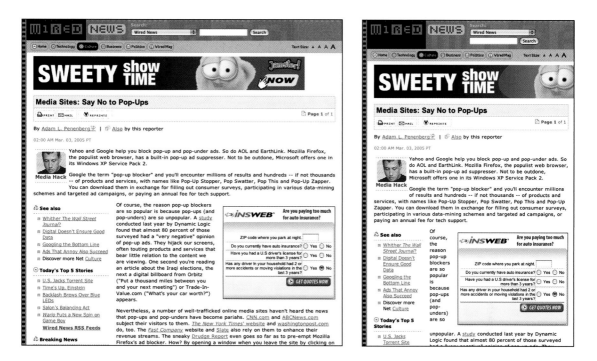

Flexibility is a basic characteristic of Web pages. For example, pages that adapt to fill the browser window are more accessible than pages that are fixed at an "optimal" width. The concept of fixed design makes no sense in the Web context, where "optimal" is influenced by so many variables—text size, browsing device, display size, window size, and so on. On the Web, the optimal design is one that adapts to the user's environment (**Figure 1.2**).

Flexible design makes sense on the Web because users have a large measure of control over their environment. Users can view pages with or without formatting, with their own preferred colors and fonts, with or without link underlines, in a wide or narrow browser window—the list goes on. The Web environment is unique in that both user and designer share responsibility for the user experience. Designers need to respect this partnership and avoid using elements such as text graphics and fixed-width pages that cannot be modified by the user.

FIGURE 1.2

The *Wired* site uses a flexible layout that keeps its integrity at different window widths.

1.1 BASIC PRINCIPLES

1.1.1 Design simply

In *Envisioning Information,* Edward Tufte says, "Information consists of *differences that make a difference*" and claims that, in conveying meaning, "the most economical means can yield distinctions that make a difference." When information is presented in its most basic form, it's easy to draw attention to aspects that are important. For example, in a block of text, emphasizing a word or phrase is a matter of changing one attribute: color, typeface, or style. In a simple layout, drawing the eye to an important section can be accomplished by changing one attribute: background color, leading, or typeface. If, however, the page already contains elements of emphasis, highlighting what is important becomes difficult since so many elements are already competing for attention. And if more and more emphasis is added in an effort to make each element stand out, the resulting design is chaotic and confusing (**Figure 1.3**).

Simple designs are not the norm on the Web. Most designs lack restraint and consequently are difficult to use and often are not functional. Working in such an environment, designers may avoid simple designs for fear of "not being flashy enough." We should take the risk and design with restraint. Flashy may be impressive but the effect quickly wears off, particularly when a flashy site is not accessible and functional. There may have been a time when people turned to the Web to be wowed, but today's Web user is looking for results. The best way to impress users is by getting them where they need to go.

Another reason we design complex pages is to gain mastery over the medium. Pixel-perfect designs are reassuring because they afford some consistency across different systems and browsers. The cost, however, is high for both the designer and user. The methods used to guarantee consistency—complex layout tables, needless images—produce pages bloated with unnecessary markup. Maintenance of such pages is painful because simple changes and updates require significant effort and may result in broken pages since one misplaced tag can send the layout into

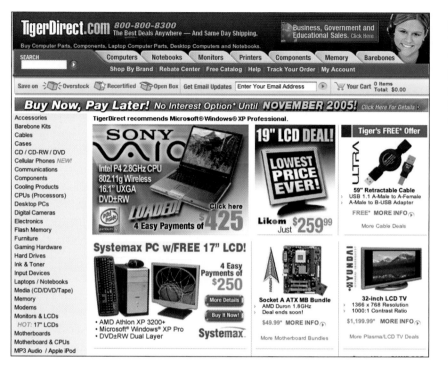

disarray. The result: pages that load slowly and are often out of date because upkeep is too difficult.

On the other hand, simple designs, using only simple structures and clean markup, have many benefits. Without needless markup, pages load much more quickly and are easier to maintain. Users appreciate clean designs that are easy to use and uncluttered. Indeed, the best designs are most noticeable in their effect: enabling users to successfully complete their task. Aim for designs that are effective, easy to maintain, and structurally sound. Ultimately, Web sites are a tool for people to use, not merely to look at. Our success lies in the user's success.

In a nutshell. Simple designs are easier to use and maintain. Design simple sites, emphasizing important elements and using simple structures and clean, standards-based markup.

1.1.2 Build well

In many ways, good Web design is simply a matter of building well. The Web has built-in elements that, when used properly, allow for user modification and support different access methods. Universal usability requires that we utilize these methods to their best advantage.

One of the Web's most basic methods for providing universal access is through alternates and fallbacks. When a user encounters content that is inaccessible in a given format, the equivalent information is provided through alternate methods. The ALT and LONGDESC attributes of the IMG tag are intended to provide nonvisual users an accessible text version of information contained in an image. The NOSCRIPT and NOFRAMES tags provide alternate access for users who cannot access JavaScript or frames. The OBJECT tag allows a layered approach to providing alternates. For example, a video might fall back on a slide show, then audio, then an image, and finally text. Effective use of fallbacks is an essential aspect of designing for universal usability (**Figure 1.4**).

Flexibility and user modification are additional inherent Web properties that enable universal access. Web pages adapt to their environment, so the same page can be viewed on a computer display, printed page, or cell phone. This flexibility allows Web pages to be read by a wide range of devices, from computers to kitchen appliances. Flexibility, coupled with user control, allows users to transform pages to meet their access requirements. Users can choose to view pages with or without styles, with user-defined styles, with large or small text, with images or without. Even the needs of an individual vary depending on many factors. For example, users may need larger text when viewing pages projected in a lecture hall, or want to disable image loading when accessing the Internet from their home computer. Universal usability is possible on the Web when pages are designed for transformation and users are empowered to control their environment.

In a nutshell. The Web has properties that enable universal access. Take full advantage of these inherent properties, such as fallbacks, flexibility, and user control, to construct universally usable Web sites.

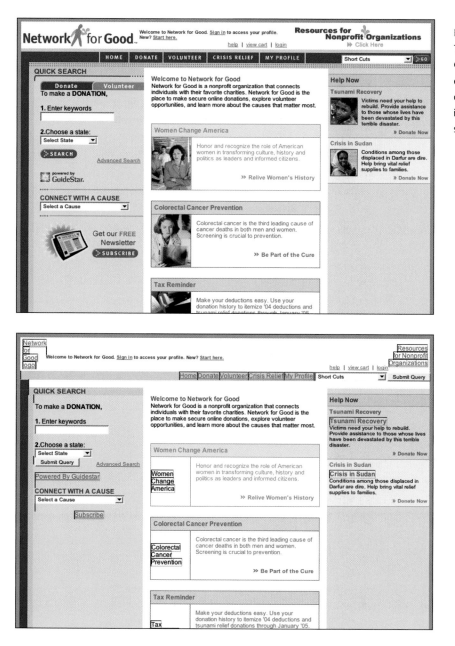

OUACHITA TECHNICAL COLLEGE

1.1.3 Favor HTML over other formats

HTML is the native language of the Web. It contains basic constructs that enable universal access because it was designed specifically for that purpose. Web access software, such as browsers, screen readers, and search engines, were written to read and interpret HTML documents. Web access has been expanded to include other formats—most notably PDF, Flash, and Shockwave. While these formats contain accessibility features, they are inferior to HTML for universal usability because key attributes, such as fallbacks, keyboard accessibility, and structure, are not as integrated as well as they are with HTML.

PDF, or Portable Document Format, allows designers to provide access to documents that exist in other formats, such as word-processing or page-layout software. Converting these documents to PDF is a way of distributing the documents without requiring users to own the originating software. Users can open PDF documents using Acrobat Reader (a free download) and other applications included in operating systems or that are commercially available. Providing documents in PDF reduces distribution overhead by not requiring conversion to HTML. In addition, documents that are saved and distributed as PDFs will retain the appearance of the originating document.

Flash, Java, and Shockwave provide interactivity options beyond HTML's forms and links. Web designers often want to offer more sophisticated interface options, such as dropdown menus and animated buttons and controls. Most games and animations rely on nonstandard formats, such as Shockwave, since the necessary level of interactivity and feedback cannot be accomplished using standard HTML (**Figure 1.5**).

HTML is not the most powerful or interactive of tools. However, from a universal usability perspective, HTML wins hands down. The Web's built-in flexibility and fallbacks are not available in other formats because these tools were not explicitly designed to provide access. Accessibility features have been added to PDF, Flash, and Shockwave. On the other hand, features such as keyboard accessibility, flexibility, and user control are inherent to the Web and are therefore addressed more effectively with HTML.

FIGURE 1.5
The Lego site provides interactive features that cannot be accomplished using plain HTML.

Designers who consider using another document format must carefully weigh the risks and benefits. Does the benefit of increased control or added functionality outweigh the risk of usability barriers? Could the control and functionality be achieved using HTML, even if the design is less streamlined or less elegant?

When an alternate format is deemed necessary, make use of all accessibility features offered by the authoring software. For example, PDF documents can be designed to contain structural markup using the tagged PDF format, and to reflow when the user enlarges text. Flash documents can contain text alternates for images and other nontext elements, and actionable elements can be made keyboard accessible. Utilize these and other accessibility features when designing content using nonstandard formats.

FIGURE 1.6

Many documents on the Copyright site are available in both HTML (1) and PDF (2) formats. Providing nonstandard formats in addition to accessible HTML enhances usability, as some users may prefer to download a PDF document for printing.

Information Circulars, Factsheets, and FLs

The circulars and factsheets below provide basic information about registration, fees, compulsory licenses, and other aspects of the copyright process.

Note: In order to view the PDF files below, your computer must be equipped with the free Adobe Acrobat Reader 6 program or other software capable of reading PDF version 1.4 files.

No.	Format	Circular Title
1	PDF, Text	Copyright Basics
1	Text	Fundamentos del Derecho de Autor (Spanish version of Circular 1)
1a	Text	United States Copyright Office A Brief History and Overview
1b	PDF, Text	Limitations on Information Furnished by the Copyright Office
1c	PDF, Text	Make Sure Your Application Will Be Acceptable
2	PDF	Publications on Copyright
3	PDF	Copyright Notice
4	PDF, Text	Copyright Fees
5	PDF, Text	How to Open and Maintain a Deposit Account in the U.S. Copyright Office

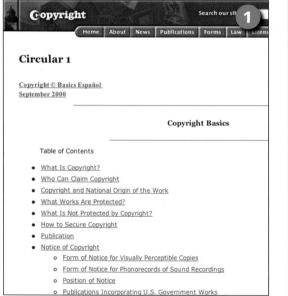

Ultimately, however, for a site to offer universal usability, its content and functionality must be provided using standard Web structures. Any use of nonstandard formats must be offered as an alternative to accessible HTML. For instance, information provided only in a PDF document will be inaccessible to some users, so the equivalent information must also be available on an accessible HTML page. This alternate approach has benefits for all users. For example, some users might prefer a PDF for printing driving directions, whereas driving directions on an accessible HTML page benefit users who cannot or prefer not to work with PDF documents (**Figure 1.6**).

In a nutshell. HTML is the best format for universal usability. Provide documents in nonstandard formats, such as PDF and Flash, only as an alternative to accessible HTML.

1.2 MARKUP

1.2.1 Design for keyboard access
One of the primary requirements for universal usability is keyboard accessibility. Some users prefer or are required to use the keyboard to operate a computer. Keyboard users include nonvisual users who cannot see the see the screen to point and click, and users who control the computer using alternate input devices, such as a switch device or voice commands. To work with Web pages, these users must be able to accomplish all tasks using the keyboard.

On the most basic level, interactive controls must be operable from the keyboard. Any time a control requires the use of a pointing device, such as a mouse, keyboard-only users are immobilized because they cannot point and click. Users must be able to select menu items, activate links and buttons, and fill in and submit form fields using the keyboard (**Figure 1.7**, *next page*).

But keyboard accessibility extends beyond functionality. Controls must be logical, self-explanatory, and must function according to user expectations.

FIGURE 1.7

The product order
page on the OXO site
has site links, a search
feature, links to other
product categories, an
order form, and more.
For universal usability,
all these functional
elements must be
accessible from the
keyboard.

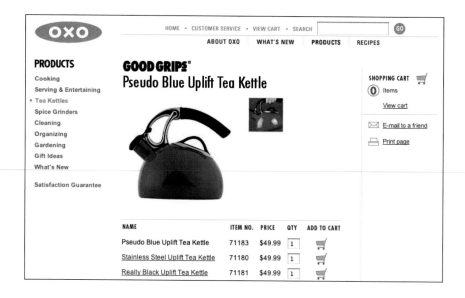

Keyboard users can use the tab key to cycle through actionable
elements on a Web page. For efficient tabbing, the "tab order" of a Web
page must follow a logical sequence. Tab order is generally determined
by the order in which elements appear in the code. While it is possible
to define tab order using the TABINDEX attribute, the best approach is
to construct pages so actionable elements follow a logical sequence in
the code. For instance, site links and section links should precede page
links, and footer links should appear last in the code. Form fields should
follow a logical and customary sequence: for example, first name, last
name, and email address (**Figure 1.8**). In addition, related elements must
be grouped: For instance, all section navigation links should be grouped
together in the code.

Another aspect of designing for keyboard access is the labeling
of interactive elements. For keyboard access, these elements must be
understandable without the surrounding context of the page, because
users may choose to access page controls directly rather than within the
page by, for example, tabbing directly to links or form elements. Self-
explanatory controls allow keyboard users to understand the purpose

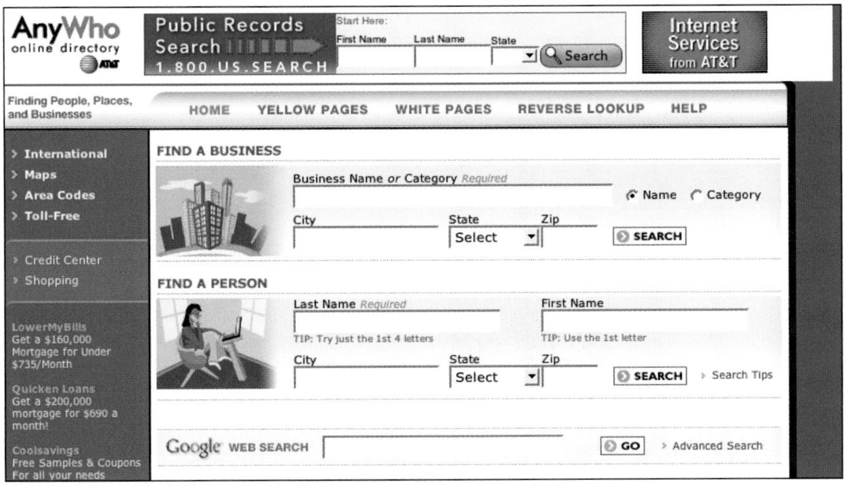

FIGURE 1.8
For keyboard
accessibility, links and
form elements must be
clearly labeled and follow
a logical sequence, as
on the AnyWho lookup
form for businesses and
individuals.

and function of each control without having to expand their focus to the surrounding context. Links that are labeled "Click here" are not self-explanatory, whereas links that are labeled to describe the target are. Form fields without labels are not self-explanatory, whereas form fields labeled using the LABEL FOR tag are. Design pages to be usable via links and form elements.

Finally, keyboard accessibility depends on keyboard controls functioning in a manner that is consistent with user expectations. Keyboard control of Web pages is based on a simple functional paradigm: Elements are selected using the tab or arrow key, and selected elements are activated using the return or enter key. Whenever controls use different event triggers—for example, menus that activate when an item is selected or buttons that respond to mouse clicks—keyboard accessibility suffers. Make sure all functional elements respond to the select-activate keyboard interface.

In a nutshell. Some users navigate the Web using the keyboard only. Make sure all functional elements, such as links and forms, can be controlled and activated from the keyboard.

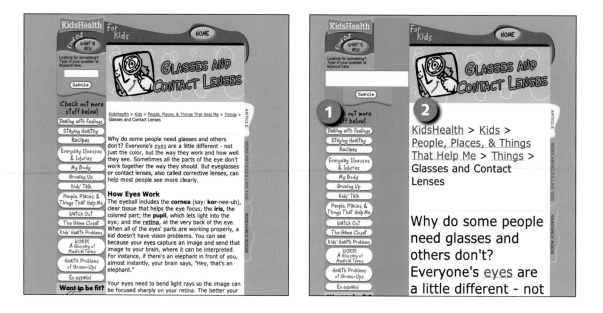

FIGURE 1.9
KidsHealth uses images for navigation and a fixed column width. When users enlarge text, the links do not enlarge (1) and the text column does not expand (2).

1.2.2 Design for transformation

A common misconception among Web designers is that Web page designs are static in the same way as a poster, book, or billboard, resulting in pages that are designed with one view in mind. These pages are generally designed for a standard screen width, text size, column width, line length, and so on. They do not hold up well when subjected to adaptations, such as enlarged type or a wide or narrow browser window. In fact, Web pages are inherently dynamic, transforming themselves to accommodate different access devices and user needs. This adaptability is what sets the Web apart for universal usability, allowing users to transform content to satisfy their needs and preferences. However, with Web pages that are designed to support only one view—pages that use fixed type sizes and column widths—adaptations are either impossible or not useful because these pages do not adapt well (**Figure 1.9**). For universal usability, designers need to support the adaptability of the Web by anticipating variation in their page designs and by creating pages that transform gracefully.

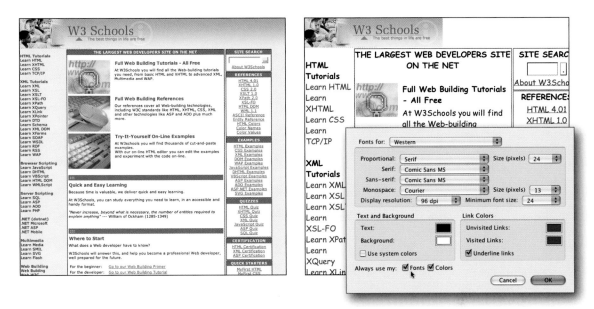

FIGURE 1.10

Users may opt to use their own fonts and colors when browsing the Web, which can dramatically alter the look of a Web page.

While the foundational aspects of a Web page are determined by the designer—for example, the order of elements in the code, the size and content of images—many of the presentational aspects, such as colors, typeface, and text size, are merely suggestions. These attributes change, depending on the device used to access the page and on the preferences of the user (**Figure 1.10**).

Color, for example, is highly unpredictable. On the one hand, users can override color settings and apply their own colors. But even when a page is viewed with its original colors, the color values vary dramatically, depending on whether the page is viewed on a cell phone, laptop, high-resolution display, or via a projector. To design for color transformation, use high-contrast colors that will hold up to variable conditions.

Page width is another common variable. In the early days of the Web, most users accessed Web pages using a desktop computer. Decisions about page width were made based on width of the smallest monitor currently in use. Today, the variety of access devices makes it unrealistic to design for a certain screen width. To design for variable screen dimensions, use flexible layouts that adapt to different window widths.

FIGURE 1.11
The IBM Ease of Use
site uses a simple,
flexible design that can
accommodate different
window widths and
enlarged text.

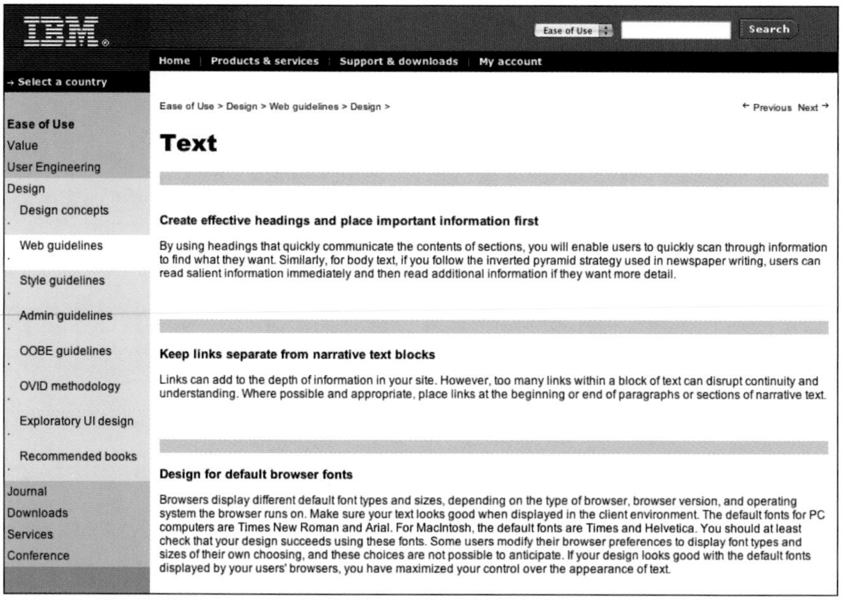

IBM.

Ease of Use

Search

Home | Products & services | Support & downloads | My account

→ Select a country

Ease of Use > Design > Web guidelines > Design >   ← Previous Next →

Ease of Use
Value
User Engineering
Design
  Design concepts
  Web guidelines
  Style guidelines
  Admin guidelines
  OOBE guidelines
  OVID methodology
  Exploratory UI design
  Recommended books
Journal
Downloads
Services
Conference

Text

Create effective headings and place important information first

By using headings that quickly communicate the contents of sections, you will enable users to quickly scan through information to find what they want. Similarly, for body text, if you follow the inverted pyramid strategy used in newspaper writing, users can read salient information immediately and then read additional information if they want more detail.

Keep links separate from narrative text blocks

Links can add to the depth of information in your site. However, too many links within a block of text can disrupt continuity and understanding. Where possible and appropriate, place links at the beginning or end of paragraphs or sections of narrative text.

Design for default browser fonts

Browsers display different default font types and sizes, depending on the type of browser, browser version, and operating system the browser runs on. Make sure your text looks good when displayed in the client environment. The default fonts for PC computers are Times New Roman and Arial. For Macintosh, the default fonts are Times and Helvetica. You should at least check that your design succeeds using these fonts. Some users modify their browser preferences to display font types and sizes of their own choosing, and these choices are not possible to anticipate. If your design looks good with the default fonts displayed by your users' browsers, you have maximized your control over the appearance of text.

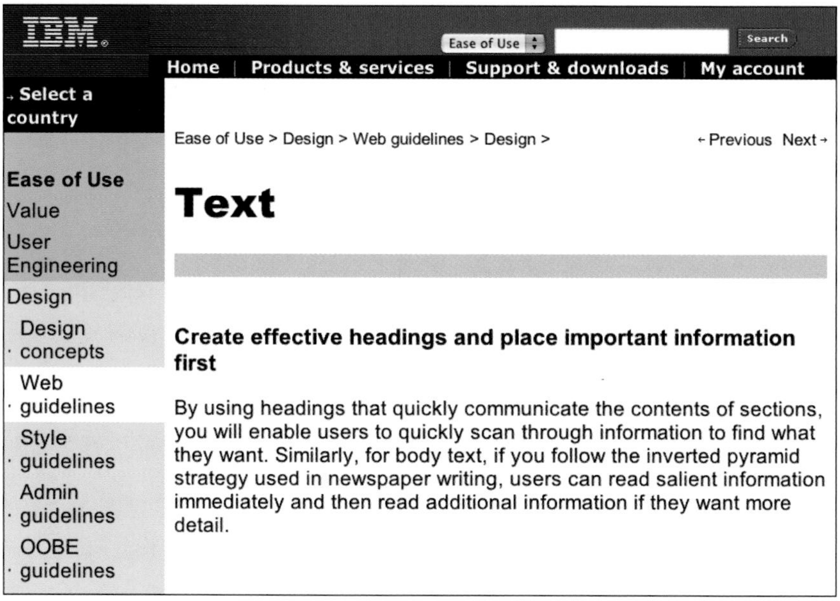

IBM.

Ease of Use

Search

Home | **Products & services** | **Support & downloads** | **My account**

→ **Select a country**

Ease of Use > Design > Web guidelines > Design >   ← Previous Next →

Ease of Use
Value
User
Engineering
Design
· Design concepts
· Web guidelines
· Style guidelines
· Admin guidelines
· OOBE guidelines

Text

Create effective headings and place important information first

By using headings that quickly communicate the contents of sections, you will enable users to quickly scan through information to find what they want. Similarly, for body text, if you follow the inverted pyramid strategy used in newspaper writing, users can read salient information immediately and then read additional information if they want more detail.

Variations in text size also influence the page design. Different browsers come with different default text sizes. Users can adjust text size using the zoom feature. In addition, display resolution settings influence the way text displays in the browser. Pages that are designed for transformation respond gracefully to variations in text size. To accommodate different text sizes, use simple, flexible layouts that maintain their integrity with enlarged text (**Figure 1.11**).

In a nutshell. Web pages adapt to the user environment and user modifications. Design pages that adapt to different conditions, such as enlarged text or different window widths, while keeping their design integrity.

1.2.3 Allow users to control their environment

On the Web, users have more control over their environment than with any other medium. Users can customize and control their interactions with Web content to an unprecedented degree. The potential for user customization offers an opportunity to redefine the relationship between designer and user.

In product or graphic design, designers make decisions on behalf of users. With user-centered design, decisions are guided by user input, observation, and feedback but the goal remains the same: to determine and implement the optimal design solution. However, even the best-researched user-centered design will inevitably fail since no design can meet the needs and preferences of all users. Each user has different needs depending on his or her environment and access method—for example, whether accessing a Web page on a large monitor or a cell phone.

On the other hand, a customizable interface allows users to control aspects of the interface. Designers are still responsible for providing well-designed pages, but these pages must be built for user adaptation. Users then have the option of changing aspects of the design to better meet their needs and preferences.

Every partnership has boundaries. On the Web, an important boundary exists between the domain of the designer and the user. The designer controls many elements of the user interface, but so does the

FIGURE 1.12

The Opera browser offers a range of viewing options (1), including the accessibility, high-contrast view shown here (2). Flexible pages, such as those on the *Fast Company* site, remain usable even with user modification.

user. Users can decide whether to open links in a new window or tab, underline links, load images, load styles, or use JavaScript. Users can customize their text settings and background colors. Users can use the style specified by the designer, or apply their own styles. Users can make their viewing window wide or narrow, tall or short. In fact, users can customize their environment to the point where a Web page bears little resemblance to its original design (**Figure 1.12**).

Conflicts arise when designers implement decisions that belong in the users' domain. Decisions made by the designer often take precedence over user settings, and users have little recourse for regaining control of their environment. For example, when a designer targets links to open pages in a new window, users have no way to open the pages in the same window. When a designer removes link underlines, users cannot reinstate them short of overriding style settings altogether. When a designer creates pages that are fixed at a certain width, users cannot make pages wider or narrower.

In general, such design decisions are intended to enhance the user experience: Opening links in a new window allows users to explore related materials without losing contact with the originating site;

removing link underlines makes pages cleaner and easier to read because underlines are distracting and interfere with letterforms; and creating fixed-width pages restricts line length so users are not forced to read long lines of text. However, each decision has the potential of causing usability problems for some users: When links open in a new window, users who rely on the back button to navigate the Web will not have access to that functionality; when links are not underlined, users who cannot distinguish colors may not be able to identify links; and when pages are set to a fixed width, users who need to enlarge text will be forced to read narrow text columns.

But most important, the user can control all these parameters. Users who prefer multiple windows can choose to open links in a new window. Users who object to link underlines can turn off underlines in their browser preferences. Users who prefer wide or narrow pages can set page width by resizing the browser window.

Well-intentioned designers make decisions on behalf of users because users do not always make good use of the elements that are under their control. While sometimes effective, this approach can introduce additional usability barriers. Universal usability requires a design partnership, where designers and users work with the elements of the interface that support user control.

In a nutshell. Web users have control over many aspects of their environment. Do not take control of aspects of the user interface, such as text size and link underlines, that belong in the domain of the user.

CHAPTER 2

Document Structure

U SERS OFTEN ENCOUNTER COMPATIBILITY PROBLEMS when working with electronic documents created on different computers because the format is tied to the software and hardware used to create the document. They may not have the software required to open and work with the document. If they are able to open the file, they may find the document illegible because they don't have the necessary fonts. The Web came into being in part to address the challenges of sharing electronic documents. HTML is a "device-independent" document format that can be read by any number of devices.

Perhaps the most fundamental attribute of a device-independent format is the ability to separate content and presentation. When content is handled separately from presentation, documents can be accessed without requiring specific fonts, operating systems, software, and display formats. Content can be read using different devices—graphical browsers, text-only browsers, speech synthesizers, printed output, PDAs, Web-enabled appliances, and so on. The actual rendering of the pages is left up to the client software.

Historically, designers avoided HTML structural elements because their display did not coincide with our design aesthetic. Instead, we used presentational formatting to gain control over visual design and layout. We used FONT and B tags instead of H1-6 tags to control the size and style of headings; we used line breaks instead of P tags to control the margin between paragraphs; we used tables to position elements on the page; we used images for page elements. This design approach became common practice, and structural markup fell by the wayside. As a result, today's Web is a vast system for exchanging static electronic documents, and not the smart, accessible Web envisioned by its creators.

Cascading Style Sheets, or css, has changed all of that. css provides the means for designers to control page display while maintaining the separation of content and presentation. Because css is now well supported among modern browsers, we can abandon old practices and begin building the Web as it was intended. Presentation markup is unnecessary, as are the workarounds we once relied on to gain control over visual design. Instead, we can build Web pages using structural html elements, and use css to design their display. We can separate content and presentation by managing content in structured html documents and presentation in style sheets.

When we manage content and presentation separately, our design decisions need not get in the way of access. Some users require access only to content. Nonvisual users, for example, do not gain from accessing presentation information. Other users need access to content with a customized display. When our pages are free of presentation markup, users can access the content—whether rendered with our styles, user-defined styles, software-defined styles, or no styles—depending on the requirements of the user.

2.1 BASIC PRINCIPLES

2.1.1 Separate content and presentation

When information is displayed on a printed page, its content and presentation are inextricably bound. The expression of the information is tied to its visual design, and the reader must be able to access and interpret the information as presented. When access is subject to requirements such as 20/20 vision, the information is bound to be inaccessible to some readers.

The Web is a medium designed to remove access requirements and to make content accessible to all. Universal access to Web content is achieved in a number of ways, one of which is device independence. With device independence, access to Web content is not bound to a certain operating system, software, or even a computer; indeed, some kitchen appliances read Web documents. Document display does not

FIGURE 2.1
Wikipedia uses structural markup to identify headings, lists, and paragraphs, and CSS to define their visual properties.

require a certain typeface, size, margins, or colors. In fact, Web content can be displayed in any size and color—the choice of display is in the hands of the user.

The key to device independence and universal access is in the separation of content and presentation. Divorcing content from presentation is a foreign concept for many of us, however. When designing a document, we are accustomed to making choices about the visual properties of elements such as headings, paragraphs, and lists. We use typography to differentiate these elements: We make headings big and bold, paragraphs indented, and lists indented and bulleted.

Web documents can be built using the same design approach—B for bold, I for italic, and so on. The notion of one static visual design, however, is contrary to the nature of the medium. Web documents are meant to adapt, providing not one view but many. They are also machine readable, and machines can't make much sense of visual markup. What does *bold* mean? What does an indent signify? Many Web functions rely on access to document structure in order to take meaningful actions with Web documents.

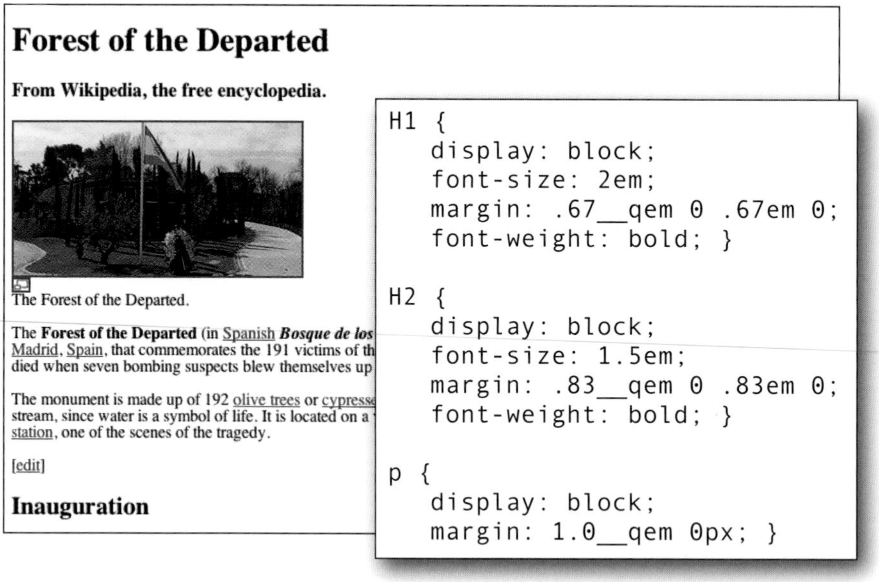

FIGURE 2.2

When structured
documents are displayed
without styles, the client
software determines the
visual formatting. Here,
the structured Wikipedia
page is displayed without
styles in Safari. Select
Safari style definitions
are shown in the inset.

Forest of the Departed

From Wikipedia, the free encyclopedia.

The Forest of the Departed.

The **Forest of the Departed** (in <u>Spanish</u> ***Bosque de los***
<u>Madrid</u>, <u>Spain</u>, that commemorates the 191 victims of th
died when seven bombing suspects blew themselves up

The monument is made up of 192 <u>olive trees</u> or <u>cypress</u>
stream, since water is a symbol of life. It is located on a
<u>station</u>, one of the scenes of the tragedy.

[edit]

Inauguration

```
H1 {
    display: block;
    font-size: 2em;
    margin: .67__qem 0 .67em 0;
    font-weight: bold; }

H2 {
    display: block;
    font-size: 1.5em;
    margin: .83__qem 0 .83em 0;
    font-weight: bold; }

p {
    display: block;
    margin: 1.0__qem 0px; }
```

Rather than building documents using visual design practices, we
need to build structure into our Web documents. Headings must be
encoded as headings, paragraphs as paragraphs, lists as lists. Creating
an HTML document is not a visual process but an intellectual one, in
which each element is identified and assigned the appropriate semantic
meaning. The resulting document is rich with meaning beyond what is
displayed on the screen, and can be rendered by any Web-enabled device
in the appropriate format (**Figure 2.1,** *previous page*).

Structured documents can be styled in several ways. Software that
renders Web pages applies styles to HTML elements. For example, the
STRONG tag produces bold text in most browsers, and EM for emphasis
produces italicized text. The visual formatting of heading levels—large
to small, bold and/or italic—is assigned using styles. Web designers
could simply develop structured documents and leave the rendering to
the client software (**Figure 2.2**).

Most designers prefer to have a hand in the visual design of their
pages, however, and CSS provides the means to control page display while
maintaining the separation of content and presentation. With CSS, we

FIGURE 2.3
When content and presentation are separate, alternate formats are easy to provide by applying a different style sheet. Through linked style sheets, Boxes and Arrows allows users to choose between regular (1), large-font (2), and print (3) versions.

can control the interpretation of the tags we use to create a structured document. We can assign font size and weight to headings, indents to paragraphs, custom bullets to lists, and more. css has far more formatting options than standard HTML presentation markup. And since content and presentation are separate, one document can have many different designs simply by applying a different style sheet (**Figure 2.3**).

In a nutshell. Content that is encoded without display requirements can be accessed by any software or device. Use HTML documents for content, and css for presentation.

2.1.2 Mark up document structure

A markup language like HTML wraps standard document elements in identifying "tags" that describe the meaning of each element, such as titles, headings, paragraphs, lists, tables, links, addresses, citations, and quotes. The resulting document is "machine-friendly"—it can be read and interpreted by software. When a document has structural markup, software can make use of it by displaying the document title in the browser title bar, by providing a list of links or headings, and so on. Screen reader software can use structure to modulate tone by reading headings more slowly than main text, or by reading links using a different voice. Search engines can index a structured document more accurately than a plain text document because phrases marked as headings help the software determine the document's subject and primary focus.

Many of today's Web documents do not contain structural markup, or they make use of only the most basic tags: TITLE, BODY, maybe a P or two. Many documents do contain structural markup, but for visual purposes, such as BLOCKQUOTE for margins and TABLE for page layout. Most other markup is presentation markup: tags that describe the visual attributes of page elements. These include such tags as BR for line breaks, FONT for setting type size and typeface, B for bold, and I for italic.

On the surface, a nonstructured document may look no different than a structured one. Whether a designer marks paragraphs with a P or two BRs (line breaks) is not visually apparent. However, the logical structure underlying a well-structured document adds a layer of meaning that gives power and utility to the Web. Software can read text documents; with structured text documents, software can both read *and derive meaning*. A truly interconnected Web requires documents that can be cataloged and connected by software. To do this well, software needs structure.

Take the title of this book. <i>Access by Design</i> is visually identifiable as a book title because it is italicized and uses title case—two conventions that denote book titles. However, software cannot recognize the phrase as a title because I means italics—nothing more. On the other

ELEMENT	USAGE
h1, h2, h3, h3, h5, h6	Headings
p	Paragraphs
blockquote	Quoted text
ul, ol	Unordered and ordered lists
table, th, tr, td	Tabular information
em, strong	Emphasized words and phrases
cite	Citations (e.g., book titles)
abbr, acronym	Abbreviations and acronyms

FIGURE 2.4
Table of common
structural tags.

hand, `<cite>Access by Design</cite>` is universally identifiable as a book title because the HTML tag CITE is used to denote citations. When a book title is tagged for structure, software can do useful things, such as scan the Web for all instances where the book is cited in other Web documents. In this case, instances marked with I would fall through the cracks.

To build structured documents, encode content using structural markup. Identify page sections—header, navigation, content, footer—and the elements contained within the sections—headings, paragraphs, lists, and tables. Instead of thinking about what each element should look like, think about what each element *is*—and tag it using the appropriate HTML structural tag (**Figure 2.4**). Avoid meaningless tags, such as FONT, BR, B, and I, and do not misuse structural tags for presentation purposes, such as tagging paragraphs with the BLOCKQUOTE tag to create margins. When it comes time to think about visual design, turn to CSS to define the appearance of structural elements.

In a nutshell. Semantic markup produces content that can be read and *interpreted* by software. When encoding content, tag the meaning of document elements using structural HTML.

FIGURE 2.5

(facing page)

CSS Zen Garden is an illustration of the range of designs that can be accomplished using Cascading Style Sheets (CSS). Different style sheets are applied to the same HTML document to produce these (and many more) distinctive pages.

2.1.3 Use style sheets for presentation

Before CSS, designers avoided structural tags because the browser, not the designer, determined their visual appearance. Browsers did not always make the most elegant decisions about formatting, creating huge headings, lists bulleted and indented, and paragraphs marked with a blank line, to name a few. To get around these defaults and to gain control over visual formatting, we constructed pages using nonstructural tags, such as FONT and B, tables for layout, and images for page elements.

These methods served the visual aspect of the Web, but at a cost. Web pages coded with presentation markup are heavy with unnecessary code. Complex layout tables are easily broken, and changes to page elements designed as images require significant effort. As a result, we tend not to make changes to sites designed this way because, like a house of cards, one small change could bring the entire design crashing down.

Now that CSS is well supported in browsers, there is no need to resort to "old-school" design methods. We can use styles to override browser formatting and to apply visual formatting to structural elements. CSS offers more control, in fact, than presentation markup—for example, typographic control over leading and tracking is available using CSS.

Style sheets offer control over nonvisual attributes as well. With aural styles, we can design the audible experience of our Web pages. For example, we can control the voice type and inflection used for reading different elements—perhaps using a female voice for links and a male voice for all other content. Another useful aural style is the "speak" style, which can be used to tell screen reader software whether to speak (XEROX) or spell out (WWW) abbreviations and acronyms.

Other benefits of CSS are consistency and ease-of-use. When content is marked up structurally, one CSS document can control the design of all linked documents. With one master style sheet, all headings share the same visual properties, all paragraphs, all lists, and so on. Changing visual attributes is easy: One small change to the style sheet is all that's needed to change the page background color, or to use a different typeface. Major redesigns can be accomplished without ever touching the content pages (**Figure 2.5**).

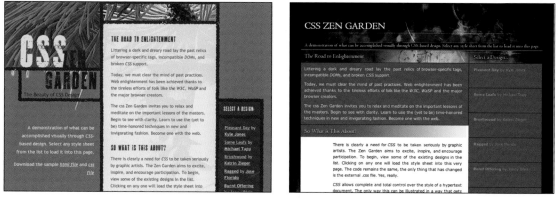

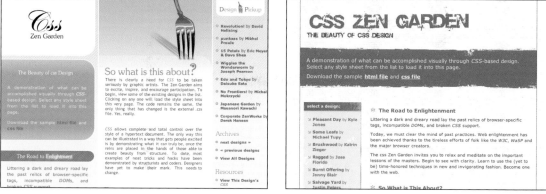

When content and presentation are separate, custom views are easy to provide by applying different style sheets. Designers can offer different versions—for example, a large-type version, a high-contrast version, a printing version, and different versions for various devices. Users with specific needs can then apply their own custom style sheet that meets their access requirements.

In a nutshell. Style sheets provide control and flexibility for designers and users. Use style sheets to control the presentation of Web pages.

2.1.4 Design pages that function without style sheets

Under some circumstances, styles may not be part of a user's experience of Web pages. Some users use browsers that do not support styles. Some users turn off style sheets or apply a custom style sheet. Nonvisual users do not access visual styles. These users may encounter difficulties if designers rely on styles, for example, to divide functional areas of a page or to group related elements. To support users who do not access styles, structured documents must be functional, comprehensible, and usable without the formatting supplied via style sheets.

For pages to function without style sheet formatting, content in the HTML document must be logical when read or viewed in sequence. The sequence of page elements must follow a logical order—for example, header, navigation, content, and footer. Moreover, the content belonging in each section must be contained within each element.

In general, pages that are structured using basic HTML tags will work best when users access them without styles, or with user-defined styles. Pages that are designed using nonstructural elements do not adapt as well as pages designed using structural elements, such as paragraphs and lists. Browser or user-defined styles and screen readers cannot account for custom elements—`<div id="banner">`, `<div id="footer">`— and will not have the means to differentiate these elements. However, if elements are designed using structural markup—`<p id="banner">`, `<ul id="footer">`—software can differentiate these elements by accessing the structural tags.

In a nutshell. Some users do not access styles. Design pages that are comprehensible and usable without style sheet formatting.

2.2 MARKUP

2.2.1 Write valid code

Building to standards means following a standard set of specifications that defines the syntax or rules for the structure of HTML or other code. One of the benefits of building to standards is that results can be measured against specifications to ensure that a project meets code. Web pages are built primarily using the standards for markup (HTML and XHTML) and presentation (CSS) developed by the World Wide Web Consortium (W3C). When Web pages are built to standards, they are more likely to function properly with browsers that also conform to specifications.

To ensure standards compliance, we need to begin each page with a DOCTYPE, or document type declaration. DOCTYPE tells software which set of specifications to use in handling pages:

```
<!DOCTYPE html PUBLIC "-//W3C//DTD XHTML 1.0
    Transitional//EN"
"http://www.w3.org/TR/xhtml1/DTD/xhtml1-
    transitional.dtd">
```

In the above example, the document type is identified (XHTML 1.0 Transitional) along with the URL for the DTD, or document type definition. For page access, DOCTYPE tells browsers which set of standards to follow, increasing the likelihood that pages will display properly across software and devices. For page validation, DOCTYPE tells validation software which set of specifications to measure against in assessing standards compliance.

In a nutshell. Valid code is essential to solid document structure. Identify document type and validate pages to ensure quality and compatibility.

2.2.2 Use linked style sheets

Style can be applied to a Web page either by including style information in the HTML document or by linking to one or more external style sheets from the HTML document. Linked styles have several advantages over embedded styles.

Linked styles save bandwidth. When style information is embedded within an HTML page, the style information must be downloaded with each page. On the other hand, linked styles are downloaded once and cached by the browser, then applied to each page in a site that references the style sheet file.

Linked styles promote consistency and reduce site maintenance workload. When all presentation information is referenced within one file, all pages share the same design. A site-wide design change, such as a different page background or font replacement, requires one change in one document, rather than potentially thousands of individual pages. This ease of maintenance clearly benefits the site developer, but users also stand to gain. Design consistency makes sites more usable and accessible because users only have to learn the user interface once to use the site. Inconsistent designs require the user to relearn the interface at each page.

Linked styles enable alternate views. We can use linked styles to provide alternate styles for different access methods: for example, the "print" media type for printed pages, or the "handheld" media type for use on small devices, such as PDAs. We can also use alternate styles to provide options for viewing our pages, such as a large-text or high-contrast view (**Figure 2.6**).

In a nutshell. Linked style sheets promote design consistency and produce faster downloads. Include style information in a linked style sheet rather than on each Web page.

CHAPTER 3

Text

Setting type on the web is fundamentally different from setting type in print. In print typography, established guidelines help us to design readable documents. Printed text is normally set to between 10 and 12 points and is black on a white background. On the Web there is no such thing as 12-point type. Factors such as monitor resolution and browser settings influence the size at which Web type displays, and most of these variables are controlled by the user, not the designer.

Web documents are flexible, particularly text-based ones. While the Web designer creates a page with a certain look and feel, the Web user has the means to adapt that view to fit his or her needs and preferences. The extent to which the user can customize the page is directly related to the degree to which the designer relinquishes control over the look of the site. Designers must embrace the variability of Web text as opposed to trying to hold it in place—for example, by fixing its size or by using graphic text. When a designer takes inappropriate measures to retain control, Web access is compromised. Web typography is not about providing one optimal view of a document; its goal is to accommodate transformation.

The Web offers a one-size-fits-all solution to text documents. But unlike the ill-fitting "unisize" shirt or sweater, the Web can actually fulfill its promise because the Web designer does not have to divine some size that will miraculously fit all people. On the Web it is the user, not the designer, who determines the fit.

FIGURE 3.1

Audible uses graphic text for navigation and content. Since graphic text cannot be customized, some users may have trouble using the Audible site.

3. 1 BASIC PRINCIPLES

3.1.1 Use plain text for text

Graphic text differs from plain text because it is composed of pixels as opposed to distinct, recognizable characters. We use graphic text for several reasons: to create visual effects, such as drop shadows or bevels; to use a nonstandard typeface; to create image rollover effects using JavaScript; or to create text that cannot be copied or resized. Graphic text is often used for site navigation, particularly on pages with fixed layouts that do not adapt well to text size changes (**Figure 3.1**).

Graphic text, however, is not customizable; users cannot resize or recolor it. A user-defined style sheet will have no effect on graphic text. If site navigation is image-based, there will be people who cannot use it, and a site without navigation is like a car without a steering wheel—you can't take it anywhere.

Graphic text has no meaning beyond its visual representation. An image of a word is nothing more than colored pixels. A graphic heading, for example, cannot be tagged as the main descriptor of content—which means that pages will not index well for searching and will not read well with screen reader software.

On the other hand, text that is really text can be sized, colored, styled, copied, pasted, indexed and searched. Text is the most powerful and accessible element on the Web. With the text styling options available using css, there is little need to use graphic text, particularly for essential elements such as navigation and content.

In a nutshell. Text has many benefits over other content formats: it can be read by software, it adapts to different user environments, and text supports user customization. Whenever possible, favor text over other content formats.

3.1.2 Use CSS for styling text

css styles contain all the details about the visual characteristics of Web pages. Designers have different methods for applying styles to pages. *Embedded* and *inline* styles are style declarations included within html documents. An *external style sheet* is a file containing style declarations that is referenced by html documents and used to render pages.

When external style sheets are used, content is stored in the html document, and presentation information is stored in the style sheet document. This separation of content and presentation makes it easy to customize the visual display—for example, by allowing users to apply their own styles. To use the Web, a user might require a high-contrast view (for instance, white or yellow text on a black background), or really large type, or some combination of color, size, and typeface. When all visual information is contained in a style sheet, the user can create a custom style sheet specific to his or her requirements and apply it to all Web pages (**Figure 3.2,** *next page*).

In a nutshell. Style sheets provide the greatest flexibility for styling and customizing text display. Use style sheets to define text's visual properties—font, size, color, and so on.

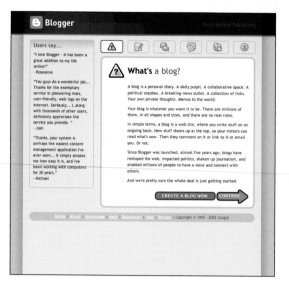 

FIGURE 3.2

Blogger uses style sheets for visual formatting. Users who need a custom view can apply their own formatting to Blogger pages, such as the large type, high-contrast view shown here.

3.2 SIZE

3.2.1 Allow user settings to define base text size

Typographic conventions tell us that the optimal text size for readability is somewhere between 10 and 12 points. Printed documents generally follow these conventions and satisfy the average reader under typical reading conditions. For the nonaverage reader, there are reading aids, such as glasses and document enlargers, or large-print editions.

The Web is different. Web users can set their browser to display text at an optimal size, based on their needs and environment. Some users require type that is larger than average for reading. Some may need to enlarge text so a Web page is readable in a group setting. Others might want the text as small as possible so they can read it on a PDA or cell phone display.

In designing text, the base text size should be a decision left to the user. All other text elements should be sized relative to the user-specified default. This approach allows users to establish optimal settings in their browser preferences and to have those settings apply on all

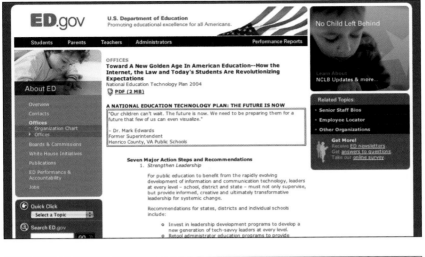

FIGURE 3.3

Ed.gov uses small text, whereas Medline Plus uses average-sized text. When pages have different base text sizes, users must adjust their text zoom for consistent readability.

sites that they visit. If each site has a different base text size, users must continually adjust their text settings as they move from site to site (**Figure 3.3**).

In a nutshell. Users should define their optimal text size setting. Allow the main text of a page to size according to the user-defined setting.

3.2.2 Size other text elements relative to the user-defined text size

Designers use size and position to convey information about the structure of a document. Headings are usually larger than the main text. Supplementary text, such as captions and footnotes, is generally smaller than the main text. These visual cues help readers negotiate the structure of the information on the page.

On the Web we can use size to define relationships between page elements without having to require specific sizes, such as 12-point type for body text and 14-point type for headings. When we use relative measurements—such as keywords (smaller, larger), percentages (90%, 110%), or ems (.8 em, 1.2 em)—to set text size variants, the main text is sized at the user-specified setting and all other text elements are sized relative to it. For example, if the user-specified text size is 16 points and we define headings using the keyword "larger," then the headings will display at approximately 18 points. This method reveals the information hierarchy on the page while allowing users to view the text at a size that is readable.

In a nutshell. Relative measurements—such as percentages and ems—size elements relative to their parent element. Use relative measurements for type variants—such as headings and links—so they size relative to the user-defined text setting.

3.2.3 Design pages that can accommodate different text sizes

Designing a Web page that is flexible and allows for customization is far more challenging than designing a static page. Fluidity is one of the most obvious differences: Print offers one view of a document; the Web offers any number of views.

When we design page layouts that require pixel-level precision, and a user requires large text, we create a point of friction between the tool and the user. If we resolve this conflict by setting type so it cannot be resized, or by using graphic text, then some users will not be able to use the site. If text can be enlarged, but doing so sends the layout into disarray, then our design suffers, and users may not be able to make sense of

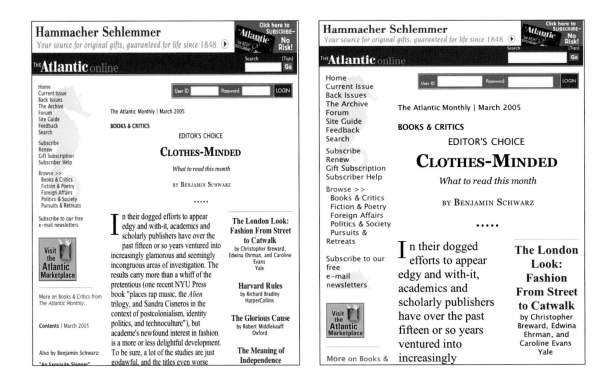

the site (**Figure 3.4**). On the other hand, a well-crafted, flexible page can accommodate different text sizes while keeping its overall integrity. When users resize text, the page and column widths expand or collapse accordingly, but the overall design—the positioning of elements, and the relationships between elements—remains intact (**Figure 3.5**, *next page*).

In a nutshell. Users must be able to resize text and still have a functional page. Design flexible pages so users can resize text without breaking the layout.

FIGURE 3.4

Fixed-width layouts, such as those on the *Atlantic,* do not adapt well because the text columns do not adjust to accommodate text size changes.

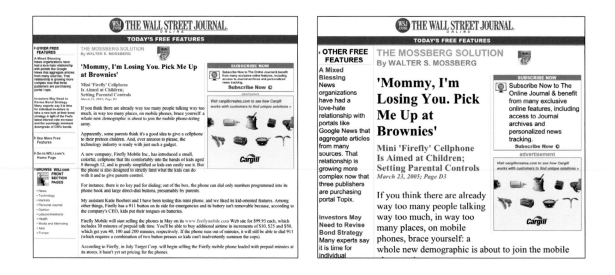

FIGURE 3.5

Flexible layouts, such as those on the *Wall Street Journal,* adapt to adjustments in type size. The columns resize and reflow when text is enlarged.

3.3 COLOR

3.3.1 Maintain contrast between text and background

One of the advantages of designing for the Web is that we can use color without dealing with high printing costs and the complexities of color reproduction. On the Web, colored text and backgrounds are easy to achieve using styles and other color settings. However, choosing the wrong colors is also easy and can reduce readability. For example, contrast between text and background is necessary for the reader to be able to distinguish letterforms. Pages with insufficient contrast can be tiring, even impossible, for people to read (**Figure 3.6**).

The biggest determiner of contrast is the brightness of a color. Black text on a white background is the ultimate high-contrast color combination because black has a 0% brightness value, whereas white has a 100% brightness value. Hue also affects legibility, with complementary hues—black and white, dark purple and light yellow—producing the highest contrast.

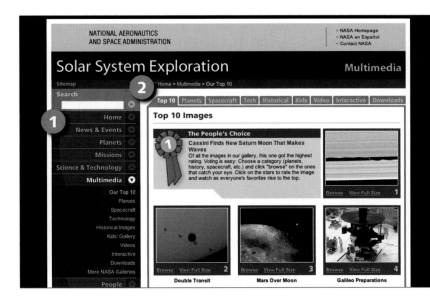

FIGURE 3.6

Some of the navigation links on the Solar System Exploration pages may be difficult to read because there is insufficient contrast between background and foreground colors. The links that are a lighter shade of the background color (1, 2) are particularly difficult to make out.

In a nutshell. Low-contrast color combinations interfere with readability. Use complementary colors and brightness values—such as black and white or purple and yellow—to produce the highest contrast between text and background.

3.3.2 Use style sheets for setting text color

Some people have certain color requirements for reading text. For example, older people might find that they read best in a high-contrast view, with white or yellow text against a black background. Others may have difficulty perceiving specific hues, or distinguishing the difference between colors of a similar hue. With Web pages, users can customize their environment so color does not get in the way.

One method for applying custom color combinations is for users to create a style sheet containing their requirements for viewing, and instruct the browser to use that style sheet on all Web pages. This method allows users to override author-defined styles and to apply style settings that reflect their viewing requirements. Of course, this method only works on pages that use style sheets and are marked up using proper

HTML code. It does no good to have a user-defined style that sets all paragraphs at 42-point type if the Web page it is applied to has no paragraphs defined, or if the background color is defined the old-fashioned way in the HTML code. On the other hand, pages that are marked up using standard structural markup will honor user-specified settings.

In a nutshell. Not all color combinations work for all users. Define colors using style sheets so people who need certain color combinations—such as white on black or yellow on black—can apply a custom style sheet.

3.3.3 Do not use text color alone to convey information

Color is a common communication device. For example, traffic signals use color to direct the flow of traffic: a red signal says stop, a green signal says go, and a yellow signal is, well, open to interpretation. However, color is a nonuniversal communication device. For color to communicate effectively, the recipient must have vision and the ability to distinguish between colors.

When color is used on Web pages for visual emphasis or as part of a directive, nonvisual users and some visual users will not see it and will miss its significance. For example, if red text identifies required fields on a Web form, then people who cannot see the colored text, or cannot distinguish it from the other field labels, may not enter the required data.

Color can be used as a way to communicate information, but it should be paired with other communication methods. For visual users, pair color with other methods—such as a different typeface or bold text for section headings—to produce typographic emphasis. For visual and nonvisual users, reinforce color with context to draw attention to specific words or fields, such as marking required fields with an asterisk or with the word *required* (**Figure 3.7**).

In a nutshell. Color is not universally accessible and therefore cannot be relied upon as the sole means of conveying information. Pair other methods—such as typography or text—with color to convey emphasis or information.

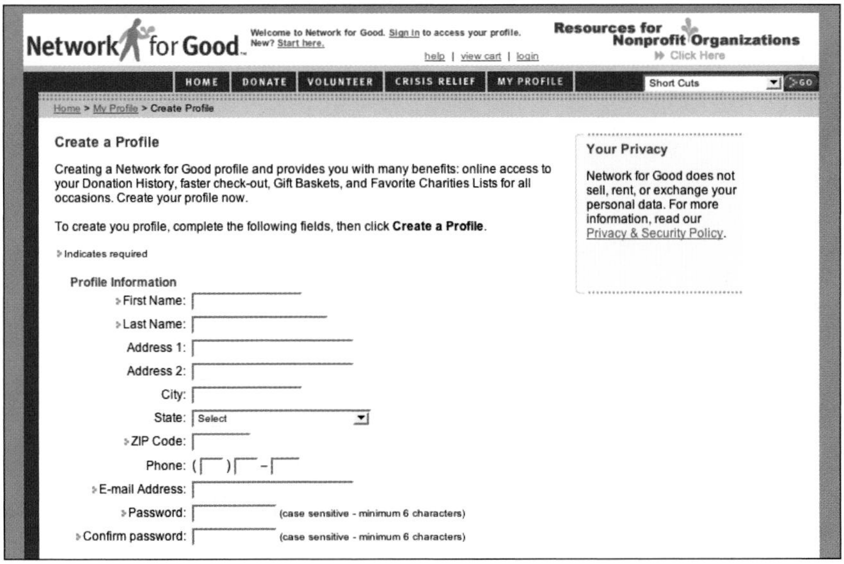

FIGURE 3.7
Network for Good uses a colored asterisk to mark required form fields. The asterisk is a graphic containing the alt-text "required," which makes it accessible to visual and nonvisual users.

3.4 MARKUP

3.4.1 Mark up text using structural tags

The Web offers a means to describe the function of text as opposed to simply defining its physical properties. A well-tagged Web document has layers of information beyond the printed page. When a printed paragraph contains a line of italicized text, the reader must determine the rationale: Are the italics intended for emphasis, to indicate a defined term, or to mark a foreign word or a citation? On the Web that same text can be tagged as EM for emphasis or CITE for citation. Basic HTML provides tags to identify structural elements such as lists, headings, tables, emphasis, acronyms, citations, and much more.

Structural markup creates machine-friendly text that can be put to many uses. For example, search engines can read heading tags, determine what a page is about, and index it accurately. Screen reader software can use markup to convey emphasis to the listener or to provide a page overview by reading only page headings. With structured documents, software could be designed to extract all occurrences of citations to generate a *Works Cited* document, or all occurrences of headings to create a table of contents. The potential uses for structurally encoded Web documents are limitless. However, for this potential to be realized, designers must employ correct, consistent use of standard Web markup.

When designing Web documents, designers should favor structural tags, such as H1–H6 for headings and EM for emphasis, over tags that only define the physical properties of a word or phrase, such as B for bold and I for italics. For instance, rather than tag a section heading as big and bold, determine what level the heading is in the information structure of the page—the main heading or some level of subheading—and mark it accordingly. Then style the heading as big and bold using style sheets.

In a nutshell. Structural markup adds meaning to documents. Use structural tags—H1–H6, P, EM, STRONG, and so on—to describe the meaning and function of text elements.

3.4.2 Use structural markup appropriately

Faced with the limited palette of HTML, designers have long been misappropriating structural HTML tags to achieve visual effects. For example, table tags are commonly put to use as a tool for Web page layout. By using invisible tables (tables without visible borders), designers can create the multicolumn layouts common in print. Site navigation links are often placed in the left cell of an invisible layout table, and page content in the right cell. Another common practice is to use the BLOCKQUOTE tag to create margins.

Then there are elements that are tagged improperly because designers object to the way the browser renders the element. For example, lists are often not tagged as lists because the designer does not want an indent, or wants to use a custom bullet, or wants no bullet at all. In these instances the solution is often to use nonstructural markup, such as line breaks, or to misuse markup, such as using tables to format a list.

These techniques undermine the power of machine-readable structural markup. When text is coded properly, software can do useful

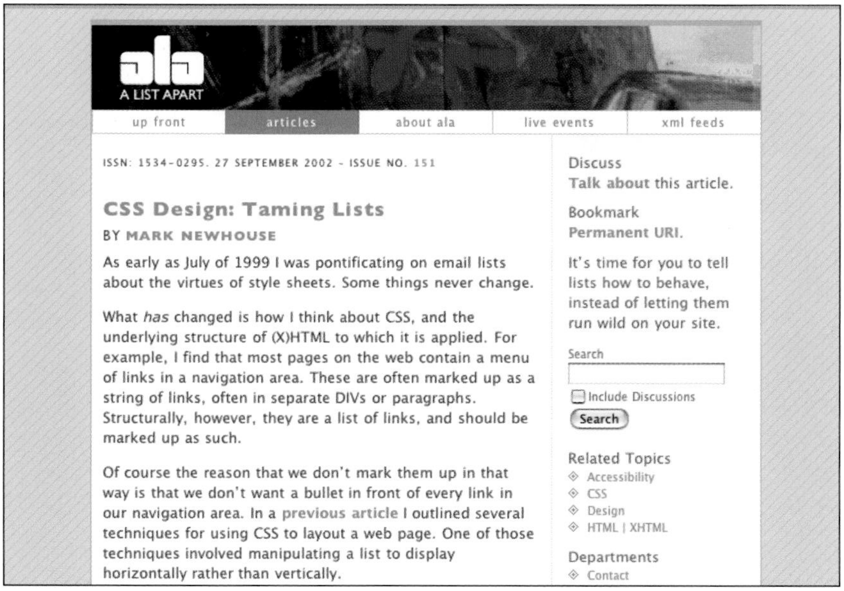

FIGURE 3.8
Navigation links on *A List Apart* are marked up as HTML lists and styled using CSS.

things with the embedded information. If, however, text marked as BLOCKQUOTE is not a quoted passage, or tables are used for both layout and data, then software can find no accurate way to make use of these elements.

Today's browsers allow designers much more control over the visual formatting of elements. With style sheets, we can control the appearance of such elements as headings, paragraphs, lists, and form fields, and create multicolumn layouts. Designers no longer need to rely on workarounds and hacks to design attractive and usable Web pages.

When marking up a text document, do not think about what the various elements should look like when displayed in the browser. Think about what each element is and tag it accordingly. Then use style sheets to define the visual properties (**Figure 3.8**).

In a nutshell. Structural integrity requires that tags be used appropriately and consistently. When marking up text using structural markup, use the tag that accurately describes the element.

CHAPTER 4

Images

Cᴏᴍᴘᴀʀᴇᴅ ᴛᴏ ᴘʀɪɴᴛᴇᴅ ɪᴍᴀɢᴇꜱ, Web images are easy to prepare and can be used without cost. However, there are drawbacks to using images on the Web. Image files are often larger than text files and take more time to download. Images command attention and can be distracting. When images are used to convey important information, people who cannot see them miss the message.

Images are not bad *per se*. Some concepts are easier to grasp when images are used to reinforce the text. For example, when assembly instructions include graphic depictions of each step, we have a way to visually confirm that we are on the right track. When product information includes a photograph, we know far more about the product than we would by simply reading a text description (**Figure 4.1**).

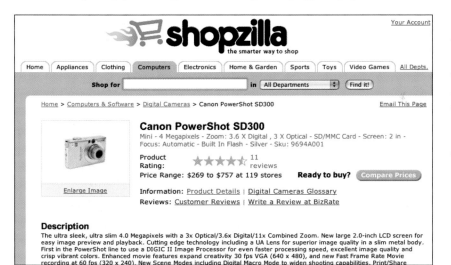

FIGURE 4.1
The Shopzilla site provides shoppers with a product image along with a text description. The image communicates information about the visual attributes of the product.

However, images affect accessibility when they are used as the sole means of conveying information. When content is presented as an image, people who cannot see images cannot access the content. People who have viewing requirements may not be able to modify images sufficiently to meet their needs. People with technical limitations—such as low bandwidth or older browser software—may not have access to images.

In some circumstances, images can be used without concern for those who cannot access them. Images are effective for establishing a visual site identity. Images and icons that reinforce text are not always essential to nonvisual users. To achieve universal usability, we do not have to abandon images—indeed, doing so would make the Web difficult for people who are helped by images. We simply need to use images appropriately, and in a way that does not result in the exclusion of some users.

4.1 BASIC PRINCIPLES

4.1.1 Use images purposefully

Some concepts require graphic representation: a chart depicting population growth on a census site, perhaps, or a photograph of a seascape on a travel site. A table of figures or a description of the scene can summarize, but cannot replace, the images. Other images are used to convey a sense of place or purpose, such as a photograph of a doctor with a patient on a hospital site. We sometimes use images as part of the user interface, such as arrows, icons, and buttons. We also use images to establish a visual identity for a site, so people know where they are. Though some of these examples are more compelling than others, in each of them the images have a purpose: providing information, establishing context, providing direction, or establishing a brand or identity.

In other cases, even though our content does not lend itself to visual representation, we feel compelled to include images because we know that "the Web is a visual medium," and we need to add images in order to "spice up our pages" (**Figure 4.2**).

FIGURE 4.2
When images are used
for visual impact, as
on the Microsoft page
shown here, their
meaning can be unclear,
as can their relationship
to the content of the
site.

This is a misuse of a powerful communication device. Images first draw the eye, then they invite interpretation. When presented with a page containing an image and text, our eye is drawn to the image. We then try to interpret why it's there and what it means. On a day-care center home page, we know that the photo of Susie and Sam on a swing is there to give us a sense of the spirit of the place, not to show us how to swing or to help us recognize Susie and Sam. When the meaning and purpose of an image is clear, images communicate extremely well. When images are unrelated, they foil all attempts at interpretation, which can lead to frustration. If the day-care center home page contained a photo of a duck, unless the center's name was something like Ducky Day Care, users might be baffled by the image.

FIGURE 4.3
Surprise.com includes
images as an essential
part of the user interface.
The meaning of the
images is unambiguous.
The images may make
features of the site more
comprehensible to users
who are helped by
images.

Images are effective when they are used purposefully. If images are not part of the message, then don't use them. When using images, make sure they are appropriate to the context. A Web page that provides computer setup information should not be peppered with photos of happy people using computers. Instead, include useful images, such as photos or diagrams that demonstrate what is described in the setup instructions (**Figure 4.3**).

In a nutshell. Images come at a cost to usability—they take time to download and are inaccessible to users who cannot see them. Use images with a purpose, such as providing information or enhancing the user interface.

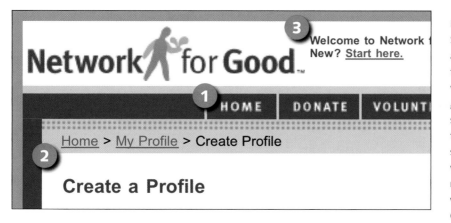

FIGURE 4.4

Some browsers, such as Opera, allow users to enlarge graphics as well as text. However, graphic text, such as the site links and logo (1) on the Network for Good site, becomes pixilated when enlarged and may be difficult to read, whereas regular text (2, 3) remains clear and legible.

4.1.2 Do not use graphic text

When it comes to advancing universal access on the Web, text is the best tool we have. Text is machine-friendly and can be read and modified by software. Text can go through many permutations and still convey its message.

Images, on the other hand, are not readable by machines and therefore are not amenable to change. From the browser's perspective, an image is a collection of colored pixels. Browser software cannot look at an image of a navigation link and recognize that the colored pixels are, in fact, text characters that make up the word *home* or *help*. As a result, software cannot make intelligent use of graphic text the way it can with plain text.

For example, the browser cannot enlarge an image gracefully; to do so intelligently, the browser would have to be able to make sense of the image. In order to make an image larger, all the browser can do is more of the same—add to the existing colored pixels—which is not an elegant solution. When a user enlarges graphic text, the result is pixilated text that is difficult to read (**Figure 4.4**).

Graphic text cannot accommodate other modifications that can be made to plain text. Users cannot change the color or style of graphic text. Applying a custom style sheet will have no effect. Moreover, people who cannot see will not have access to graphic text.

Ultimately, graphic text can be an insurmountable barrier to people who are attempting to use the Web. If images are used for navigation, people may not be able to access the information that is contained in the images. If people cannot use a site's navigation, they cannot use the site. Plain text is always better, particularly for something as essential as navigation.

Of course, sometimes graphic text is acceptable—when its purpose is visual, as in a banner graphic and logo. Here the primary function of the text is branding, not information. In these cases, the page structure (title tag, page heading) must describe the content and origins of the page, so the information conveyed in the graphic text is available to people who cannot see the image.

In a nutshell. Graphic text is not machine-readable, flexible, or customizable, and therefore is inaccessible to some users. Avoid using graphic text; use plain text instead.

4.1.3 Avoid animated images

If images are a powerful force in commanding the attention of the user, moving images are many times more commanding. It is nearly impossible to ignore a page element that is moving, particularly one that is blinking rapidly on and off.

Animations are generally seen as an annoyance on Web sites. They make it difficult to focus on the primary content of a page. For some people, animations are more than an annoyance. They cause discomfort or even medical consequences, such as migraines or seizures. Even static images that only *appear* to be animated can be a trigger—for example, images with closely spaced stripes that seem to vibrate (**Figure 4.5**).

Do not place an animation alongside primary content. An animation should appear on a page of its own so the decision to view it is an explicit user choice. Do not begin playing the animation right when the page loads. Instead, provide controls for starting and stopping the animation. Avoid images that include patterns that seem to animate, such as striped or patterned backgrounds.

FIGURE 4.5
About.com uses a
patterned background
that appears to vibrate,
which can cause
discomfort and impair
readability.

In a nutshell. Animations are distracting and can even be debilitating. Avoid using animations. When using animations, allow users to control playback: play, pause, and stop.

4.2 TEXT ALTERNATES

4.2.1 Provide alt-text for all relevant images

Many HTML structures allow designers to provide information in more than one format so users can access it using different methods. Link underlines are an alternate method for identifying links for people who cannot see color. Alternate text is an alternate method for supplying information to people who cannot see images.

When an image is essential to the content and functioning of the page, nonvisual users can read the text description provided in the ALT attribute of the IMG tag. Take a text graphic with alt-text that is the same

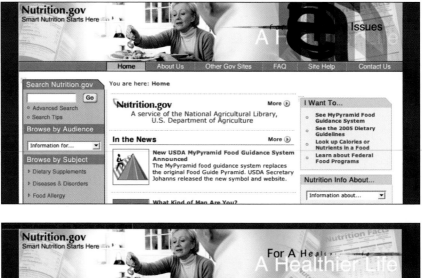

as the text that is displayed in the graphic: The visual user reads the text in the text graphic (as long as it is readable); the nonvisual user has software that reads the text in the ALT attribute (**Figure 4.6**).

When images do not contain alt-text, users who cannot access images are stuck. People who do not load images are unable to navigate a Web site that uses images for navigation if alt-text is not provided. Since screen reader software cannot interpret images, it relies on alt-text to communicate image information to the user. When an image is provided without alt-text—for example, <img src="photo.jpg">—the

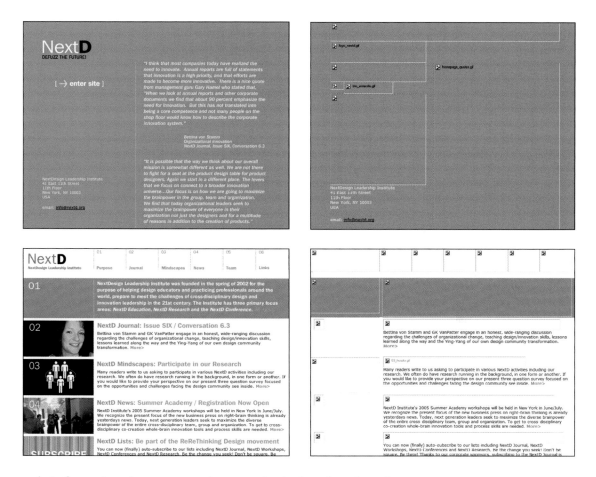

only information the screen reader can relay is that there is an image on the page and that its file name is "photo.jpg" (**Figure 4.7**).

If a picture is worth a thousand words, then a short description in the ALT attribute is a poor substitute. In many cases, however, such a description can provide enough information to assure Web access to nonvisual users. For images that are part of the user interface, provide alternate text that provides the equivalent function. In other words, the alt-text for the *New York Times* masthead should be "The New York Times masthead"; the alt-text for a print icon should be "Print

FIGURE 4.7

The NextD site uses images for essential elements but, in some instances, provides unhelpful alt-text and, in others, provides no alt-text. Users who do not access images will have trouble using the site.

this page." When an image is part of the content of the page, the alt-text should describe the image: "Photograph of sunset," "Graph of net gains," "Painting of Venus by Botticelli."

Other types of image elements should have alt-text as well. For example, image maps should have alt-text for all the active areas. Form buttons should also have alt-text. Background images cannot contain alt-text, so make sure background images are not required content.

In a nutshell. Users who cannot access images can get the equivalent information via alt-text. For images that are part of the user interface, use alt-text to provide the functional equivalent, such as "Go to next page" or "Print this page." For content images, use alt-text to provide a brief image description.

4.2.2 Provide a full text description for content images

Generally, the best that alt-text can do for content images is provide a brief description of the format and subject of an image. To fully describe the information contained in an image to a nonvisual user, we need to use other methods.

HTML allows for a full description of image content by providing the LONGDESC attribute of the IMG tag. The content of LONGDESC is a file address pointing to a file that contains a text description of the image. When a nonvisual user encounters an image with a linked text description, he or she loads the linked file, reads the description, and then returns to the originating page.

Another way to provide a full image description is to provide image captions. This approach benefits both visual and nonvisual users because text may prove helpful in comprehending the image. For example, an image caption explaining the contents of a graph or chart allows non-visual users to access the information via the caption, and helps visual users to better their understanding (**Figure 4.8**).

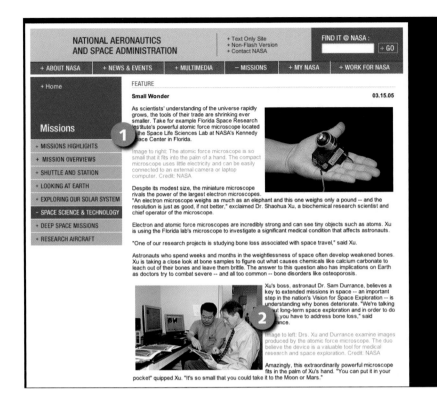

FIGURE 4.8
NASA includes captions (1, 2) for the images on its site. The captions provide information about images for both visual and nonvisual users.

In a nutshell. Content images may require more description than can be provided via alt-text. Provide a text description of the image information using a linked page or image caption.

4.2.3 Provide blank alt-text for irrelevant or redundant images

Alt-text is a way of communicating *relevant* information contained in images to people who cannot access images. However, not all images are relevant to nonvisual users. When images are relevant only in a visual context, provide blank alt-text (alt="") so nonvisual users do not have to bother with irrelevant content. Software that reads Web pages understands that empty alt-text identifies an image that is irrelevant, and so it does not communicate any information about the image to the user.

FIGURE 4.9

When images are used to reinforce text links, such as the icons on the Creative Commons site (1), alt-text is redundant since its function is handled by the link text (2). In these cases, the best approach is to provide blank alt-text (alt=" ").

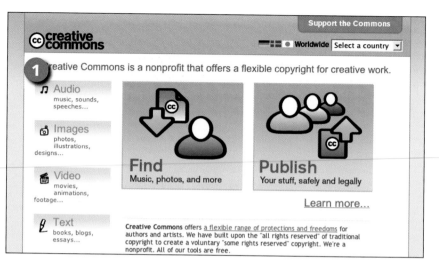

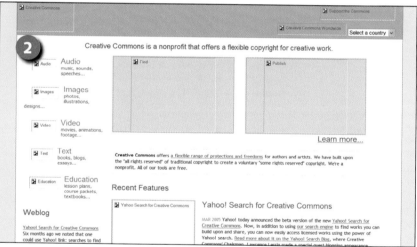

For example, elements such as spacers, bullets, and arrows do not add anything beyond visual emphasis and do not need to be described. People using screen reader software do not need to know that red bullets mark list items. When blank alt-text is used for such images, the software will skip over the image.

Also, images that appear alongside text to provide visual emphasis or clarification need not be communicated to nonvisual users. For example, text links are often paired with icons to help people quickly identify the link purpose, such as an arrow next to a "next page" link, or an email icon next to an "email this article" link. In these cases, the text link does a sufficient job of conveying the link function to nonvisual users. Generally, when images are used to reinforce text links, providing the functional equivalent via alt-text only results in redundancy (**Figure 4.9**).

In a nutshell. Not all images are relevant to nonvisual users. When images are not relevant outside of a visual context—such as spacer images or custom bullets—provide blank alt-text (`alt=""`).

4.2.4 Maintain a catalog of image content

Web designers have a lot to keep track of with respect to images. Publishing Web images involves both the visible properties of an image and its nonvisible properties—such as alt-text and long descriptions. In order to ensure quality and consistency, keep some sort of catalog of image content. When image cataloging is part of the Web design process, the task of composing alternate text becomes a deliberate part of providing image content. When an image is used in multiple locations, the catalog can be the source for the alternate text.

In a nutshell. Alt-text and text descriptions are integral to providing image-based content. Maintain an image inventory that includes alt-text and text descriptions, particularly for large-scale or collaborative projects.

4.3 SIZE

4.3.1 Keep image dimensions as small as possible

From a data perspective, images are much less efficient than text. A photograph of a toaster requires more disk space to store and more bandwidth to deliver than a paragraph of text describing the toaster.

400 × 500 high-quality JPEG = 28KB

400 × 500 low-quality JPEG = 12KB

FIGURE 4.10
Compression reduces file size, but also reduces image quality. An alternate method for producing small image files is to reduce image dimensions. Smaller images make smaller files and adapt better to different displays.

300 × 375 high-quality JPEG = 20KB

200 × 250 high-quality JPEG = 12KB

However, for the visual user, an image can be far more efficient at conveying what that toaster looks like. We use images because they are a powerful and effective way to communicate. For Web designers, the goal must be to capitalize on the advantages of images without overburdening the user.

Web images are demanding because they require more data than text. The commonly used Web image formats are bitmap images, which, unlike text and vector graphics, are not stored intelligently and therefore require more data. To make up for this, Web bitmap images, including GIF, JPEG, and PNG, use different compression schemes to reduce file size, so the images can traverse the network more quickly.

Images are also less flexible than text. While text can reflow to fit different display devices, images cannot. This means that a user viewing a 500-pixel-wide image on a 320-pixel-wide display device will be unable to see the entire image at once.

To make the best use of images, keep the image dimensions as small as possible. When it comes to file size and display speed, small images fare better than large ones (**Figure 4.10**). Also, smaller images work better on small display devices.

When saving images, use the image format that best suits the image. GIF and PNG work well for graphics and illustrations; JPEG works well for photographs. Use as much compression as possible to reduce the file size without overly degrading image quality. For GIF images, one of the

FIGURE 4.11

One way to reduce file size when working with GIF images is to reduce the number of colors used to represent an image. Often, reducing the number of colors has little noticeable effect on image quality.

256 color GIF = 36 KB

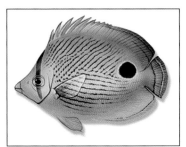

64 color GIF = 24 KB

32 color GIF = 20 KB

best ways to reduce file size is by reducing the number of colors in the image (**Figure 4.11** *previous page*).

In a nutshell. Large images take longer to download and limit page flexibility. Keep image dimensions as small as possible, and save images using as much compression as possible without significantly degrading image quality.

4.3.2 Use thumbnails for large images

Sometimes images need to be big. Product images must be large enough to display the details that are important to shoppers. Images for printing must be large enough to use in printed publications. Content images, such as those on museum or teaching sites, must be large enough to represent the content.

However, given the demands that images place on the user, large images should not appear on the main pages of a site. Most users will not want to wait to load a large image in order to move around a site. Instead, provide access to large images via a thumbnail or text link on a main page that invites the user to load the full-size image (**Figure 4.12**).

In a nutshell. Large images are sometimes integral to the purpose of a site. Provide access to large images using thumbnails or text links so users can choose whether to load the image.

CHAPTER 5

Data Tables

Tables are an html structure designed to present information in tabular format. Table markup has several components and attributes that can be used to identify the elements in a standard data table: column headings, row headings, caption, and content summary. When these elements are used properly, a data table can be understood by both visual and nonvisual users.

However, tables are often pressed into service for other purposes, including page layout, alignment, and spacing. Invisible tables (`<table border="0">`) are commonly used to create multicolumn layouts that display consistently across browsers. When table markup is misused in this way, documents become less machine-readable. Software cannot read a document accurately when its semantic meaning has been diluted with meaningless tables.

On the other hand, when table markup is used appropriately and correctly, software can read table structure. For example, screen reader software offers a table navigation option that allows users to move to a cell and hear its contents read aloud along with its column and row headings. Without correctly coded structure, however, the user will hear *only* the contents of the cell without the context provided by the headings.

Given the limitations of the medium—low resolution, limited and variable display—simple tables fare better on the Web. The primary concern with data tables is that users can easily become disoriented. Visual users may find it difficult to decode data when column headings are offscreen. Nonvisual users access each table element individually and do not have the means to orient themselves visually.

FIGURE 5.1

The Bronx Zoo pages are divided into sections—a site banner and site navigation across the top of the page, section navigation links in the left column, and the main content in the right column—using a layout table.

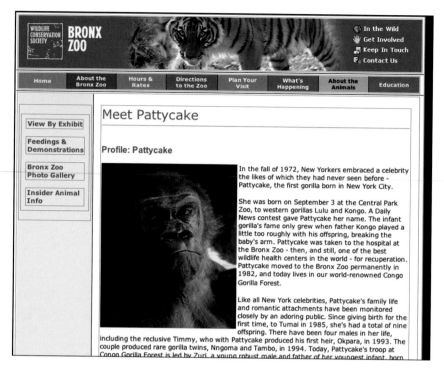

5.1 BASIC PRINCIPLES

5.1.1 Use table markup for data

Before styles were implemented and supported by client software, Web designers had no tools for laying out Web pages. HTML is not a tool for design and page layout; it is for defining document structure. As such, it is composed almost entirely of structural elements, with very few tags to describe visual properties. With the early versions of HTML, visual representation of structure was defined largely by the client software: for example, headings big and bold, quotations indented, and paragraphs separated by a blank line. Following strict HTML coding meant that Web designers really had very little chance to *design* their pages. With few options and little control, Web designers began to be creative in their use of HTML structures.

FIGURE 5.2
NPR uses CSS to design
its multicolumn layouts.

Courtesy of NPR®

For example, no structural element exists to mark a banner or navigation bar. Yet these elements are commonly used on Web sites to establish site identity and to offer navigation links to other pages in the site. One common approach to producing this familiar layout is to use table markup to divide the page into different areas (**Figure 5.1**).

The trouble with this practice is that semantic markup, such as the tags used to describe tables, is intended to describe the *function* of elements. When these tags are misused, documents are no longer machine-readable in a way that is accurate and meaningful. Software cannot distinguish "real" tables from layout tables and will try to make sense of content that is within a table.

Before css, table markup was the only option for laying out Web pages; this is no longer the case. Style sheet positioning is widely supported by client software and is a far better tool for Web page layout (**Figure 5.2**).

In a nutshell. Structural integrity requires that tags be used appropriately. Avoid using tables for layout; use tables to mark up tabular information.

FIGURE 5.3

W3Schools uses tables to provide details in its Web tutorials. On this page, rather than present all XHTML standard attributes as one complex, multidimensional table, the attributes are broken down into categories and presented in simple tables.

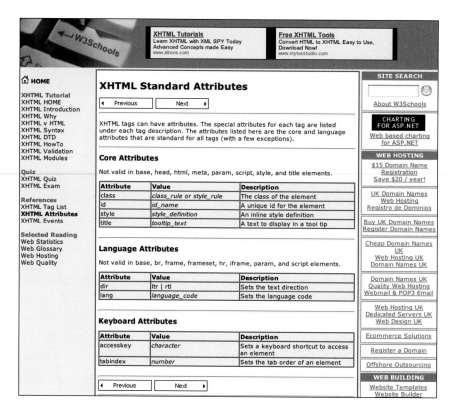

5.1.2 Simplify data table layouts

One of the more cumbersome aspects of Web documents is the scroll. With longer documents, users have no means of viewing a complete document, short of printing. Instead, pages must be viewed in segments. When documents are divided in this way, users may find it difficult to keep track of context, and may have to resort to scrolling up and down between sections (the equivalent of flipping between pages) to get a complete picture of the information.

When getting information from a table of data, context is essential. A cell of information has little meaning without the column and row headings that describe it. When we work with tables printed from spreadsheet or word-processing applications, these essential elements can be printed on each page. On a Web page, complex or lengthy tables will sometimes display with headings offscreen, or print with headings on a separate page.

When accessing tabular information, nonvisual users rely on software to provide context. A properly coded table enables software to announce the column and row headings that are associated with a table cell. However, a complex table with multiple dimensions and spanned columns or rows can be difficult for software to interpret effectively.

In general, the best way to design tables for visual and nonvisual users is to simplify the layout as much as possible. A simple table will be easier to scan, and easier for software to interpret. Rather than represent many information layers in one table, break the information into separate tables with a maximum of two dimensions (one row of column headings, one column of row headings) in each table (**Figure 5.3**).

In a nutshell. Complex data tables can be challenging to navigate for both visual and nonvisual users. Present tabular information in its simplest form for easier scanning and screen reader access.

5.2 MARKUP

5.2.1 Identify data table row and column headings

Imagine a table with no column or row headings. Each table cell would exist without context, making it difficult, if not impossible, to make sense of the information presented (**Figure 5.4,** *next page*).

Nonvisual users have a similar experience when tables are presented without properly coded row and column headings. When table cells are not explicitly tied to descriptive text, the best that software can manage is to infer that the first row and first column are headings.

The simplest way to bind headings to table cells is to use the SCOPE attribute of the table header tag (TH) to make the relationship between headings and data explicit. When coding a column or row heading, adding the SCOPE attribute declares all cells below (`<th scope="col">`) or to the right (`<th scope="row">`) as belonging to that heading.

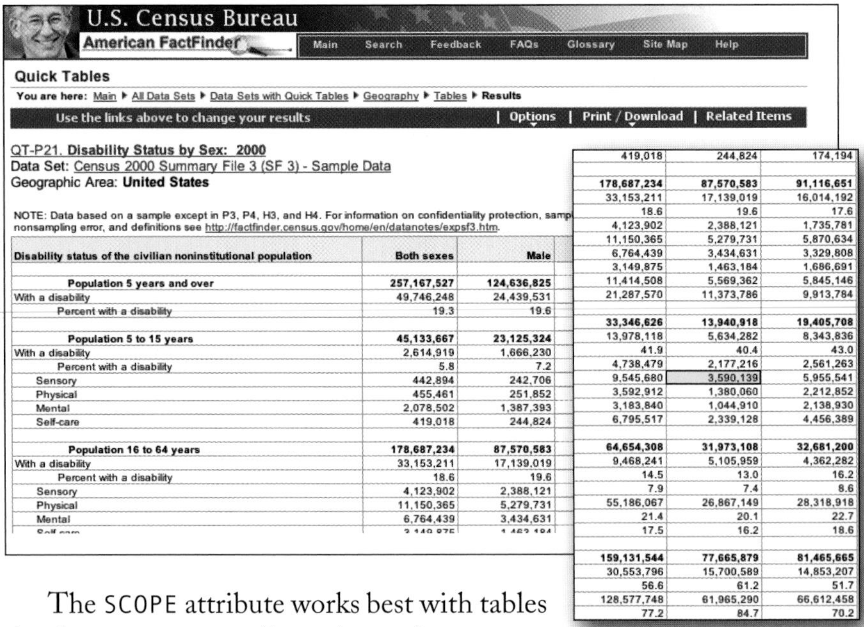

FIGURE 5.4

Data has meaning when it is presented in context, as in this data table from the U.S. Census Bureau. The numbers in the table cells have little meaning without the associated column and row headings, as demonstrated in the inset.

The SCOPE attribute works best with tables that have one or two dimensions—just one set of column headings and one set of row headings. For more complex tables, there are other methods for assigning headings, but they may not have the desired effect. Complex tables are generally difficult to decipher, and even a properly coded complex table may not be usable. Rather than tackle a complex table with complicated table code, try instead to simplify the table layout (**Figure 5.5**).

In a nutshell. Table headings are essential for establishing context for the data contained within the rows and columns of a table. Code tables so row and column headings are explicitly tied to the data they describe.

5.2.2 Use CAPTION and SUMMARY to describe data tables

In addition to headings, HTML provides two other ways to describe tabular information: CAPTION and SUMMARY. A table caption is a short title that describes the subject of the table. Captions display with the table they describe and can be formatted using CSS. A summary is a nondis-

Disability status of the civilian noninstitutional population

POPULATION 5 YEARS AND OVER

	Both sexes	Male	Female
Total	257,167,527	124,636,825	132,530,702
With a disability	49,746,248	24,439,531	25,306,717
Percent with a disability	19.3	19.6	19.1

POPULATION 5 TO 15 YEARS

	Both sexes	Male	Female
Total	45,133,667	23,125,324	22,008,343
With a disability	2,614,919	1,666,230	948,689
Percent with a disability	5.8	7.2	4.3
Sensory	442,894	242,706	200,188
Physical	455,461	251,852	203,609
Mental	2,078,502	1,387,393	691,109
Self-care	419,018	244,824	174,194

FIGURE 5.5
One approach to presenting complex data is to simplify its presentation. Here, the Disability Status table is broken into separate tables representing each population group. These simplified tables can be coded using basic table tags—CAPTION, TR, TH, and TD—and using SCOPE to associate headings and data.

playing attribute of the TABLE tag that summarizes what is described in the table. Since SUMMARY does not display, its practical purpose is to provide nonvisual users with a brief description of the subject and format of a data table. When both SUMMARY and CAPTION are present, screen reader users can orient themselves prior to working with a data table.

In a nutshell. Provide additional context by using CAPTION and SUMMARY tags to tie descriptive information about data tables to the tables they describe.

Layout Tables

T ABLES AND THEIR ASSOCIATED TAGS are HTML's tools for presenting information in tabular format, such as spreadsheets, timetables, and reports. To fully describe tabular information, the TABLE tag comes with associated elements and attributes, including the TH element to indicate column and row headings, the CAPTION element to provide a title, and the SUMMARY attribute to provide a short description of a table's purpose and structure.

In the early days of the Web, lacking more suitable options, designers adopted tables as a tool for page layout. By setting the table border value to zero (<table border="0">), the resulting "invisible" tables could be used for multiple layout tasks, such as creating columns and indents, controlling spacing, and limiting line length (**Figure 6.1**, *next page*). In fact, layout tables are so commonplace that most Web authoring tools generate tables to produce layouts.

As browser support moves more in compliance with Web standards, workarounds like layout tables become unnecessary. Presentation tags like FONT, B, and I went out the window once styles could be used for Web typography. Layout tables will suffer the same fate once CSS can be used reliably for page layout.

In the meantime, layout tables may sometimes prove necessary. Tables are more stable than styles for layout, particularly on older browsers with poor or no support for style sheet positioning. When a design requires consistency across operating systems and browsers, and compatibility with older browsers, a layout table may be a designer's only recourse.

For the most part, visual users are unaffected by layout tables, though complex layouts using nested tables take longer to load and are easily broken by one errant tag. Layouts that rely on fixed-width tables are

FIGURE 6.1

This IBM page uses layout tables (outlined in red) to divide the page into sections: banner (1), search (2), navigation links (3), content (4), and sidebar (5).

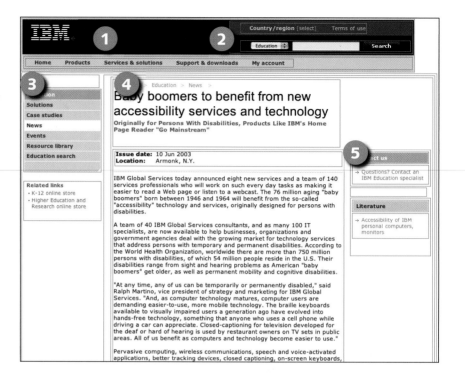

another potential problem. When table cells are set to specific widths, pages do not adapt to different display devices.

But for nonvisual users, layout tables can present problems. Software cannot easily distinguish between layout tables and data tables. When page content is contained within a table, software will attempt to make sense of it within a table context, particularly if structural elements—such as column or row headings—are used. In addition, tables can cause content fragmentation. Software reads Web content in the order that it appears in the code. If related content is divided between table elements, or among tables within tables, it may lack coherence when read in sequence.

In general, page layout is best handled using css. When layout tables are required, simple layout tables with only the most basic table tags are the least obtrusive.

6.1 BASIC PRINCIPLES

6.1.1 Use tables for layout only when necessary

Before the advent of style sheets, tables were a Web designer's only means for page layout. Without tables, only the simplest page layouts were possible. Elements could not be placed in different locations on the page, only displayed in a vertical sequence down the page.

In casting about for options, designers discovered that the structural element TABLE could be used for layout by setting its BORDER attribute to zero (`<table border="0">`), thereby rendering the table invisible. By putting page content into different table cells, pages could be divided into sections with elements positioned on different areas of the page. Table layout changed the basic character of the Web; in fact, this work-around proved so successful that most Web sites are designed using tables (**Figure 6.2,** *next page*).

However, when structural elements are used incorrectly, the utility of the Web is compromised. While the visual aspects of the Web tend to take center stage, much of its utility lies in what goes on behind the curtain. The Web is a *web* because its documents are structured—they are not simply text, but rather text with meaning applied through HTML markup. Structured documents can be read and their meaning derived by software. The most obvious benefit of structured documents is their ability to be indexed—and consequently discovered—using search engine software. However, this benefit is undermined when documents do not contain structural markup, or contain structural markup that is applied incorrectly.

When tables are used for page layout, software that reads Web pages encounters table markup and attempts to interpret the page within a table context. In the case of a screen reader, the software announces the presence of a table on the page and describes its attributes, which might sound something like "table with four columns and two rows." The software has no way of knowing that the table is not *really* a table—that its purpose is visual layout, not data presentation—and is largely irrel-evant to the nonvisual user.

FIGURE 6.2

On today's Web, table layout is the most common method for designing Web pages. Indeed, most popular Web sites use tables for layout.

Broadly speaking, whenever markup is used improperly on Web pages, the Web is weakened. Since structured documents are its basis, the Web is less robust—less effective—when structures are misused. On the other hand, pages that are coded properly strengthen the Web. The Web is at its best when structural markup is used to mark up page elements and css is used to position the elements on the page.

Implementing a layout using css can be difficult, particularly for complex, multicolumn designs. css support is inconsistent across

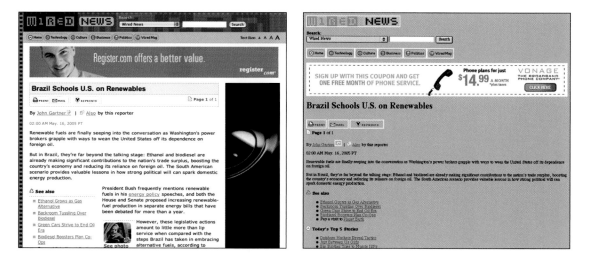

browsers, so a layout that works perfectly in one browser may look a mess in another. Older browsers do not offer sufficient css support to accurately reproduce css layouts. To use css for page layout, designers must create designs that can withstand a degree of variation among browsers and accept that pages will look unstyled in older browsers (**Figure 6.3**).

It may be that project requirements do not allow for the level of compromise that comes with css layout. For example, if a large percentage of the audience uses older, noncompliant browsers, css layout may not be an option. When consistency and backward compatibility are required, layout tables may be the only remedy. In these cases, minimize the affect of table layout by following the guidelines below.

In a nutshell. Table markup is designed to describe tabular data and not for laying out pages. Use style sheets for page layout whenever possible; fall back on table layout only as a last resort.

6.1.2 Use simple layout tables

A basic layout table with two or three columns is a mild but not insurmountable barrier to access. While screen reader software may announce the presence of the table and describe its attributes, the table

FIGURE 6.3

Layouts designed using style sheets do not always fare well in older browsers. Here, the Wired page displays without styling on Netscape 4.7 on the Macintosh. In some cases, CSS-based designs break when viewed in older browsers.

FIGURE 6.4

The multi-column layout on the Lonely Planet home page is accomplished using multiple layout tables, outlined here in red. Complex layouts with multiple rows, columns, and nested tables can cause usability problems, particularly for screen reader users.

is not likely to prevent a user from working with the page. On the other hand, a complex layout table with nested tables and multiple rows and columns will likely cause problems for screen reader users (**Figure 6.4**).

Users viewing a rendered page in the browser are not likely to notice complex tables, except at page-loading time; pages with complex layout tables take longer to display. However, nonvisual users cannot ignore complex tables. These users are not working with the rendered page but with the underlying code. When content is contained within multiple cells of a layout table, or within multiple nested tables, the software needs to account for all of the tables since table markup, *when applied to tabular elements,* is necessary for nonvisual users to access tabular information. It may be difficult for nonvisual users to distinguish tables that are relevant from those that are not. Additionally, confusion may arise when content that belongs together does not appear together in the code. Since page

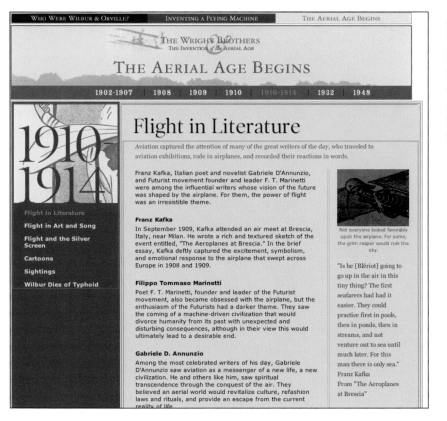

The online Wright Brothers exhibition from the National Air and Space Museum is designed using simple layout tables (outlined in red).

content is read in sequence by software, connections between related content may be lost if content is scattered among different table cells.

When using layout tables, avoid unnecessary complexity. Distill designs down to the simplest table possible (**Figure 6.5**). If a design calls for multiple table elements, nested tables, or spanned columns or rows, go back to the drawing board. Simplify the design so it can be built using a single-row, two- or three-column layout table.

In a nutshell. Layout tables can be disorienting for nonvisual users when related elements are spread across table rows and nested tables. Design simple layouts using simple layout tables.

6.2 MARKUP

6.2.1 Use only basic table tags

Part of the problem with layout tables is that nonvisual users cannot ignore them. Since tables are a structural element, they must be accounted for when they appear on the page. Table markup is important when working with tabular information, particularly for nonvisual users. The tags and attributes associated with the table element allow nonvisual users to understand and navigate information presented in tabular format. With one element (TABLE) used for two quite distinct purposes (layout and data), and with no markup to distinguish between the two, nonvisual users have little choice but to pay attention to each table. Since layout tables are so prevalent, some screen reader software manufacturers have programmed their software to differentiate between layout tables and data tables. For example, software may decide a table is for layout if it has only one row, or is without row or column headings. When software identifies a layout table, it can ignore the table attributes and read the contents of the table in the order it appears in the code.

Layout tables should only make use of the most basic row and cell markup (TR and TD). Headings, captions, summary—all the elements that describe a data table—are meaningless in the layout context. If these elements are present, software that reads Web pages may try to make logical sense of the layout table by, for example, associating cells with headings.

In a nutshell. Screen reader software cannot distinguish between "real" tables and layout tables, making table markup difficult for nonvisual users to ignore. Make layout tables as unobtrusive as possible, using only basic table tags, such as TR and TD.

6.2.2 Design layout tables for linear access

Since nonvisual users access Web pages via the underlying code, the order in which elements appear in the code greatly influences these users' experience of Web pages. Software that reads Web pages *linearizes*

1 National Park Service
U.S. Department of the Interior

2 CAPE COD NATIONAL SEASHORE
MASSACHUSETTS

Cape Cod National Seashore comprises 43,604 acres of shoreline and upland landscape features, including a forty-mile long stretch of pristine sandy beach, dozens of clear, deep, freshwater kettle ponds, and upland scenes that depict evidence of how people have used the land. A variety of historic structures are within the boundary of the Seashore, including lighthouses, a lifesaving station, and numerous Cape Cod style houses. The Seashore offers six swimming beaches, eleven self-guiding nature trails, and a variety of picnic areas and scenic overlooks.

DID YOU KNOW

- Cape Cod National Seashore was authorized by act of Congress in 1961.
- Cape Cod is the largest glacial peninsula in the world, and the Great Beach, on the Atlantic side of the Cape, is the longest expanse of uninterrupted sandy shoreline on the East Coast.
- Cape Cod is composed almost entirely of material deposited by glaciers that retreated about 14,000 - 18,000 years ago. Wind and water reworked these sediments to create beaches, spits, marshes, cliffs, and dunes. Coastal processes such as tides, winds, storms, and longshore sediment transport continue to shape and reshape the area.
- The seashore receives 4.4 million total recreation visits annually.

DON'T MISS ATTRACTIONS

- Cape Cod National Seashore is to be experienced and enjoyed in any number of ways. Drive scenic roads through local towns that offer insight into past and present life on Cape Cod. Visit one of our six magnificent beaches that provide year 'round opportunities for exploration. Walk miles of nature trails through distinct habitats, or bicycle paved paths that offer numerous views. Stop at a visitor center, or enjoy fishing, birdwatching, taking photographs, and touring historic buildings.
- On Thursdays in July and August park interpreters and volunteers bring to life an exciting era of Cape Cod's maritime history. This is the 24th year that park staff have interpreted the Beach Apparatus Drill, originally performed by the men of the US Life-Saving Service to maintain their rescue readiness. Park staff don surf whites and carry out the drill to 1902 specifications. The program is just one of the many Ranger-led programs in the park.
- Visitors to the former Marconi Station Site can stand near the spot where young Italian inventor Guglielmo Marconi made communication history 100 years ago. In January 1903, the transmission of the first public two-way wireless message between Europe and America occurred. Communiqués between President Theodore Roosevelt and King Edward VII were translated into international Morse Code at Marconi's South Wellfleet and English stations, and were transmitted across the Atlantic.
- The sweep of a beam of light across a dark night sky is an experience long remembered. Visitors to Cape Cod National Seashore can view nine lighthouses, including the Nauset Light, the Three Sisters, and Highland (Cape Cod) Light, all open for viewing.

3 PHOTOGRAPHS:

4 LINKS:

Cape Cod National Seashore Home Page»

Partnering & Managing for Excellence Report»

FIGURE 6.6
Software reads Web page elements in the sequence that they appear in the code. Simple layout tables, such as those used on the National Park Service pages, read well because elements are grouped in the code and follow a logical sequence. Here, the sequence is banner (1), content (2), photos (3), related links (4), and footer (not shown).

tables—it begins reading the content in row one, column one, and moves through the table in sequence. Layout tables can cause problems when related content is broken into different rows and cells, or put into tables within tables, such as when column headings are in one row and the content they describe in another. When the table is rendered for visual display, the related content comes together on the page. When the page is read aloud, the content is fragmented and does not make sense. The headings are read together instead of with their associated content.

Since both visual and nonvisual users read Web pages, we need to design code as well as visual display. Pay close attention to the sequence of content as it appears in the code. The order and grouping of elements should mirror the order and grouping of elements on the rendered page. When using layout tables, keep related elements in the same row and cell so they are together in the code (**Figure 6.6,** *previous page*).

In a nutshell. Software reads page elements in the sequence that they appear in the code. Make certain the logical information flow of the rendered page—banner, navigation, content, and footer—is reflected in the code.

6.2.3 Use flexible cell widths

In concept, Web pages are flexible documents that adapt to fit whatever method or device is used to access them. Type size is flexible: Users can adjust text to a comfortable size. Colors are adaptable: Users can define colors according to their needs and preferences. Page layouts are intended to be flexible so they expand or collapse to fit the users' display.

In practice, many of these flexible elements are nailed into place using various coding strategies. One of these strategies is to use fixed measurements to define layout dimensions. Using pixels to define table and cell widths results in pages that will not reflow to fit different displays. This method gives designers control over aspects such as positioning, line length, and line wrapping. Unfortunately, fixed layouts constrain the power of the Web by producing documents that are designed for only one view. With so many different ways to access Web pages and possible adaptations that can be made, a single view of a Web page is simply not possible. Web pages must be flexible to accommodate different access methods.

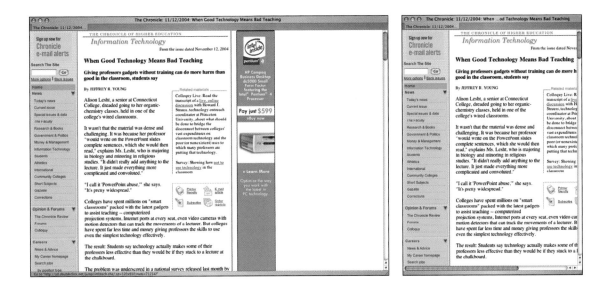

With flexible layouts, designers have less control over page elements. For example, control over line length is less reliable in a flexible layout. Flexible pages viewed on a large display may have wide columns of text that are difficult to read, whereas a fixed-width layout allows designers to set line length at a comfortable measure.

One rationale for a fixed-width page comes from print design, where factors such as optimal line length are important. With a printed document, readers cannot adjust column width, which leaves it up to the designer to provide a text size and measure that is comfortable for "normal" readers (generally thought to be between 45 and 75 characters per line). Since the medium is fixed, however, the inevitable result is that readers who do not fit the norm will be unable to read the document.

On the Web, print conventions can get in the way. With a fixed-width column, a 60-character line could become a 20-character line when a user enlarges text. Additionally, fixed-width pages are not adaptable. A fixed-width page on a large monitor makes use of only a portion of the available display area; on a small display, users may have to scroll horizontally to see the full contents of the page (**Figure 6.7**).

FIGURE 6.7

Fixed-width tables have the benefit of controlling aspects of the design, such as line length. However, fixed pages do not adapt to different window widths. Here, *The Chronicle of Higher Education* uses a fixed-width layout table for its pages. On a large display, a significant portion of the screen goes unused. On a small display, users must use the horizontal scroll to read the articles.

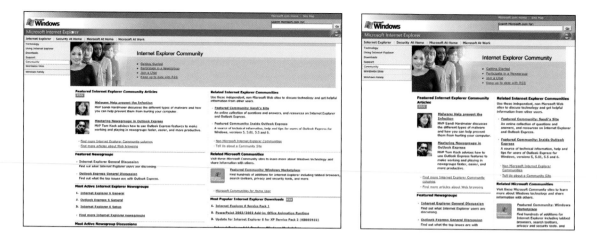

FIGURE 6.8

Microsoft uses flexible layout tables on some of its pages. The pages expand and collapse to fill the browser window.

Flexibility is a fundamental attribute of Web pages and is necessary for universal access. Web pages must be flexible to work with different software and hardware, and to accommodate a range of user needs. Don't try to restrain the inherent flexibility of Web pages through fixed layouts. Instead, use flexible layouts to build pages that adapt to different viewing conditions (**Figure 6.8**).

To create a flexible layout table, use relative measurements to define cell widths. Relative measurements, such as percentages, will cause pages to adapt to different window widths. Assign cell widths using CSS, not HTML. Not only does this practice separate content and presentation, assigning table attributes in style sheets paves the way for a later conversion from table layout to CSS layout.

In a nutshell. Flexible layouts adapt to different viewing conditions. Use flexible measurements—such as percentages—to specify the width of table cells so pages will adapt to accommodate different displays and text sizes.

CHAPTER 7

Frames

FRAMES-BASED PAGES ARE NOT STANDARD Web pages; they are
meta-documents that split the browser window into sections, pull-
ing standard HTML documents into each section, or *frame*. Frames-based
sites have advantages, though they generally favor the designer, not the
user. Site maintenance is easier because standard site elements—such as
navigation—can be handled by just one document. Design consistency
is easier to achieve with frames for the same reason: one or two files can
manage the user interface for an entire Web site.

The shortcomings of frames surface when they are considered from
a user's perspective. In some respects, frames-based pages are easy to
use. Site design is generally consistent, which makes it easier for users
to learn a Web site. When site navigation is in its own frame, users
can scroll though content without losing sight of navigation options.
However, frames-based pages function differently than standard Web
pages; essential browser functions—like printing, bookmarking, and
browser-based navigation—do not behave according to expectations.
Printing a frames-based page creates a printout of whichever frame currently has focus, which might happen to be the banner or navigation
frame, not a content frame. A bookmark to a frames-based page links
to the original meta-document, even if the user wants to return to a
page several links deep in the content frame. And the ever-popular back
button moves the user back in the frame rather than back in the page.
These inherent usability concerns make frames a construct generally to
be avoided.

When frames are used, nonvisual users and users who cannot access
framed content encounter particular problems—though some of these
can be addressed using proper HTML coding. Nonvisual users do not

have access to the visual cues that differentiate frames. When information about each frame is provided in the frame title, nonvisual users can understand the functional purpose of each frame and navigate among them. Users without access to frames can still access site content if navigation links are provided in the NOFRAMES tag. Content within the NOFRAMES tag displays when frames are disabled or unavailable, so users without frames can use those links to gain access to site content.

7.1 BASIC PRINCIPLES

7.1.1 Avoid using frames

Frames should be avoided because of the usability problems they create. Frames-based pages behave differently from standard Web pages, affecting essential Web functions such as printing, bookmarking, and navigation. General usability suffers when functions do not behave as users expect.

For example, printing a frames-based page can produce unpleasant results. The browser prints the contents of the frame that has focus when the print function is invoked, which may not be the desired outcome if it's the navigation or site banner frame.

In addition, functions that involve addressing, such as bookmarking, do not work well when frames are in use. The actual file at the URL location of a frames-based page is called a *frameset*, which contains references to one or more Web pages (**Figure 7.1**). When a user clicks a link and loads a new page in a frame within a frameset, the URL within that frame changes, but the frameset URL remains the same. If the user chooses to create a bookmark to the page in its current state, the bookmark captures the URL of the frameset's original links rather than the current state the user is viewing.

Another usability concern is the unexpected behavior of the back button. When frames are used, going back moves the user back in the frame rather than back a page. This can cause confusion if the user thinks of the frameset as a page and expects the back button to go back to the previous page.

FIGURE 7.1
Frame-based pages are composed of different Web pages loaded into separate frames. NextD uses frames to divide the page into three sections: the top frame for branding and site navigation (1), the left frame for section navigation (2), and the right frame for content (3).

Add to these usability flaws concerns directly related to access, and frames become an even less attractive design solution. Since frames-based pages are a pairing of two or more pages, users need to be able to identify the function of each frame and to navigate between frames. Nonvisual users cannot access the visual cues that help visual users differentiate frames and identify their functions. If frames are not described in the frameset code, nonvisual users cannot easily determine the function of each frame, nor can they navigate between frames. In addition, users can opt not to view frames, or they can use a browser that does not support the display of frames. These users will not have access to site content unless access is provided via the fallback NOFRAMES tag.

In general, the accessibility concerns associated with frames can be addressed using proper markup. However, even if users can access the content in a frames-based Web site, they will encounter the usability flaws inherent to frames. For this reason, frames should be avoided as a tool for Web site design.

In a nutshell. Standard behaviors—such as printing, bookmarking, and returning to a previous page—behave differently with frames-based pages than with standard Web pages and therefore cause usability problems for all users. Avoid using frames.

7.2 MARKUP

7.2.1 Use frame titles to identify the function of each frame

For visual users, frames on the page are plain to see. Often, a page is split into three frames: a banner frame, a navigation frame, and a content frame. These frames are visually differentiated by their content: the banner is generally graphical, the navigation is generally a list of links, and the content is generally a block of text and images. In addition, the browser divides frames visually via borders and scroll bars. Thus, the purpose and function of each frame is apparent to visual users (see **Figure 7.1,** *previous page*).

Nonvisual users cannot orient themselves using visual cues. Fortunately, HTML provides a method to communicate the function of each frame to nonvisual users through the TITLE attribute of the FRAMESET tag. The frame title is used to describe the frame function: for example, title="banner", title="navigation", title="content". When the frame title is present, software can provide the information so nonvisual users know the current frame and its purpose. When frames are titled, users can jump directly to the desired frame. In general, TITLE helps nonvisual users navigate between frames without becoming disoriented.

In a nutshell. Nonvisual users may have difficultly navigating a frames-based page without some idea of the contents and function of each frame. Use frame titles—such as "Banner," "Navigation," and "Content"—to label each frame so nonvisual users can differentiate and navigate between frames.

7.2.2 Provide an alternative to frames

Some browsers do not support frames. Some users opt to disable frames in their browser preferences. When users without access to frames encounter a frames-based page, the content is unavailable. Fortunately, HTML offers a fallback option, the NOFRAMES tag, which allows designers to use frames while providing alternative access to site content. Content contained within the NOFRAMES tag displays when frames are not accessible (**Figure 7.2** *next page*).

As mentioned above, frames are meta-documents made up of several HTML documents. The frames might call up the documents "banner. html", "navbar.html", and "content.html", and display these three documents using the frameset document "index.html". Users without access to frames cannot access the banner, navigation, or content because the frameset calls for these documents to be displayed simultaneously. However, using the NOFRAMES tag, we can add accessible content that will display when the page is viewed without frames.

The NOFRAMES tag accepts any HTML code, so theoretically we could duplicate all the framed content—banner, navigation, and content—within the NOFRAMES tag. However, this approach is impractical. It requires duplicate content, results in large files, and, after all, why design framed pages if we can present all the information without frames? The best use of the NOFRAMES tag is to provide access to the site content, and the best way to achieve this is to provide access to the site navigation. Including site navigation links in the NOFRAMES tag allows users to gain access to the content pages.

When content pages are accessed outside the context of frames, users may be disoriented or dead-ended if the pages do not contain identifying information or links to other pages in the site. This can occur

FIGURE 7.2

The Computer User
High-Tech Dictionary
uses a frames-based
interface to provide
access to content, but
also provides equivalent
access via a NOFRAMES
version for users who do
not access frames.

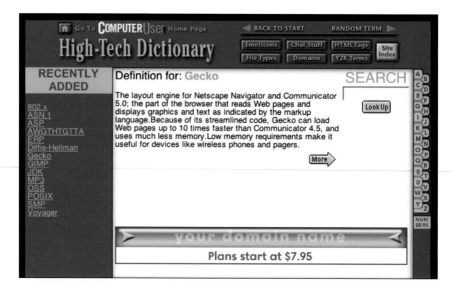

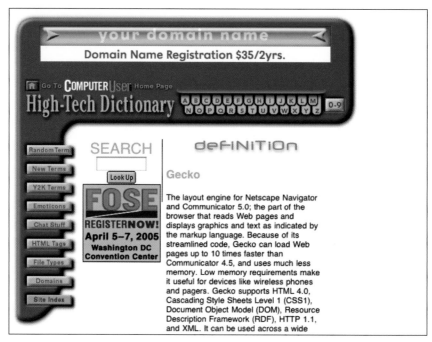

when users access content pages via a NOFRAMES link, or when users gain access directly to a content page URL via a bookmark, or as the result of a search query. Content pages that are intended to be part of a frameset are often orphaned without the surrounding frames that identify the page origins and navigation options, leaving users with no idea where they are and nowhere to go. For this reason, always include a link to the home page on content pages that are part of a frameset so users who access these pages directly can orient themselves and access additional content.

In a nutshell. Some users opt not to use frames or to use a browser that does not support frames. Use the NOFRAMES tag to provide alternate access to framed content: for example, provide access to site navigation via the NOFRAMES tag.

Lists

T HE WEB IS FULL OF LISTS, including elements that we might not normally think of as lists, such as navigation. A *navbar* is essentially a list of links. Indeed, most navigational elements could be considered lists from a structural standpoint. In addition, Web text is peppered with lists because they are easy to scan. Users can form an overview and find information more quickly when it is presented in list format.

Visual users have cues that provide context for lists. Lists are often set off from surrounding text with spacing and indents. Items customarily appear one to a line, preceded by a bullet or number. These markers tell visual users where a list begins and ends, and delimit each item.

These visual attributes can be established without list markup. Spacing and indents can be accomplished using styles or table markup; numbers or bullets can be plain text. In fact, nonstandard lists—such as navigation bars, tabs, or breadcrumbs—are commonly coded using methods other than list markup. In these cases, visual users might not experience usability problems since list items are still visually distinguished. However, nonstructured lists are not as machine-friendly as structured lists, which means nonvisual users may encounter difficulties.

When lists are marked with list markup, nonvisual users have a way to identify them. Screen reader software can announce a list, tell the user how many items are in the list, and read off each list item individually. When lists are coded using other methods, however, this contextual information is not available to the user.

Providing context works best with simple lists. For visual users, it may be possible to effectively communicate multiple levels of information using indents and other visual formatting. For nonvisual users, nested lists may be disorienting.

FIGURE 8.1

Salon.com uses images
and tables to design
the site navigation links
across the top of the
page.

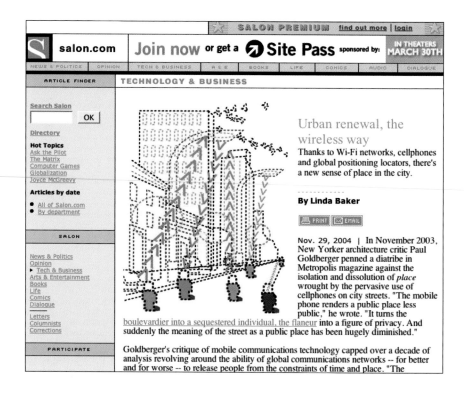

8.1 BASIC PRINCIPLES

8.1.1 Use list markup for lists

As Web designers, we are asked to define the semantic meaning of elements that we would otherwise take for granted. For example, though we use lists regularly—shopping lists, mailing lists, to-do lists—few of us have ever pondered what a list *is*. This analysis is important to our work. Well-designed Web sites have properly identified page elements.

So, what *is* a list? A list is a set of items that share a purpose and/or have common characteristics. For example, a shopping list is set of items to be purchased at the store. A mailing list is a set of email addresses. A to-do list is a set of tasks that need doing. On the Web, the most common list is for navigation. Web navigation design is a primary area of

focus for Web designers, and with good reason. To be successful, a Web site must enable users to make their way around the site and quickly locate what they are seeking. This usability requirement places demands on navigation design that, before CSS allowed designers control over structural elements, were not well met using standard list layout. For this reason, Web designers have generally avoided list markup for navigation, preferring such methods as images and tables (**Figure 8.1**).

However, now that CSS text formatting is widely supported, navigation can be well-designed using list markup and styles. With CSS, designers can overlay common navigation styles, such as tabs and button bars, onto standard HTML lists. The list styling options are many, which means designers can use a variety of style attributes to differentiate types of navigation (**Figure 8.2**). Styles even accommodate behaviors such as rollover effects—visual highlights that occur when the cursor is positioned over a link. Styles make it easy to create a link highlight that would otherwise require convoluted methods, such as images and JavaScript.

FIGURE 8.2

The Motley Fool uses lists to mark up its navigation links, and styles to design them as tabs. The inset shows the unstyled list.

In a nutshell. Lists are a common element in Web page designs—most notably, navigation is a list of links. Use list mark-up for lists and use style sheets to control their visual properties.

8.1.2 Avoid compound lists

Compound lists contain multiple levels of classification. For example, a compound shopping list has items organized by category: deli, dairy, produce, etc. With compound lists, relationships are shown visually using indents and different item markers (bullets, discs, etc.).

Compound lists may be difficult for visual users to decipher if the visual cues are insufficient. Also, compound lists may be disorienting for nonvisual users. Nested lists are coded so child lists are contained within the associated list item of the parent. On our shopping list, the parent list dairy contains a child list of milk, butter, and cottage cheese:

```
<ul>
<li>Produce</li>
<li>Dairy
   <ul>
   <li>Milk</li>
   <li>Butter</li>
   <li>Cottage cheese</li>
   </ul>
</li>
<li>Deli</li>
</ul>
```

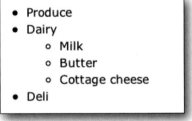

With all items coded as list items, it may be difficult for nonvisual users to differentiate between parent and child items. A better approach might be to define relationships between items using a combination of structural elements. One approach is to break the compound list into sections and mark each section with a heading:

```
<h2>Produce</h2>

<h2>Dairy</h2>
<ul>
<li>Milk</li>
<li>Butter</li>
<li>Cottage cheese</li>
</ul>

<h2>Deli</h2>
```

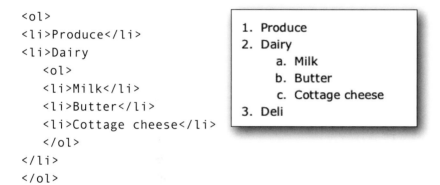

Another approach is to use ordered lists to indicate the relationship between elements:

```
<ol>
<li>Produce</li>
<li>Dairy
   <ol>
   <li>Milk</li>
   <li>Butter</li>
   <li>Cottage cheese</li>
   </ol>
</li>
</ol>
```

In a nutshell. Compound lists can be disorienting and difficult to decipher, particularly for nonvisual users. Break compound lists into sections marked by headings, or use numbering to indicate the relationships between list items.

Forms

W<small>E REGULARLY ENCOUNTER</small> and fill out forms—to apply, register, enroll, order things, and the list goes on. Forms are often poorly designed: overly complicated, nonintuitive, and redundant. As a result, we often make mistakes in completing them. We overlook important elements or mis-enter information and we generally do not enjoy the task. This holds true both on paper and on the Web.

Form design is clearly an area where functionality wins the day. Forms do not need to be visually appealing or cleverly worded; users do not expect to be delighted or entertained. Forms are a device for collecting information, and any enjoyment comes from ease of use and successful completion.

Forms should follow a logical and predictable flow, by beginning with personal information—first name, last name, birth date, gender, marital status—followed by contact information—address, phone number, email address. Users should not have to enter the same information more than once. Form fields should be clearly labeled, and fields that require information to be entered in a certain format should be clearly indicated.

Forms can have many different elements: labels, input fields, checkboxes, radio buttons, and dropdown menus. Each element in isolation does not have much use or meaning: what use is a form field without a label, or a label without a form field? The relationship between elements is what provides meaning and logic to a form and helps guide the user through to completion. For visual logic, we generally group related elements. Using proper HTML form tags, we can explicitly code the relationships between elements so nonvisual users can understand and complete forms.

FIGURE 9.1
MapQuest allows users
to enter state and
province codes directly
rather than choose them
from a dropdown menu.
Users who need a code
can reference a code
list (1) from a popup
window (2).

But even a well-designed form built using good, solid HTML may sometimes be inadequate. Forms should not be the sole means for users to communicate with companies, individuals, and organizations represented on the Web. Users should be given an alternate mode of contact for the times when forms fail or do not meet user needs.

9.1 BASIC PRINCIPLES

9.1.1 Design simple and clear forms

After links, forms are the controls we use most frequently to interact with the Web. As with links, forms need, above all else, to be operable. An operable form is one that can be completed successfully without error, with ease and minimal frustration. If a user can successfully place an order, apply for an account, or request information, then the form design is successful.

An important aspect of form design is labeling. Form elements must be clearly labeled so users know what information is required. Good labels help users understand what information to provide and reduce the margin for error. Appropriate use of form elements is also an important factor. Designers often use form elements such as dropdown menus to ensure data integrity, such as by having users choose their country from a menu rather than typing it into a text field. However, dropdown menus can become unwieldy when there are more than 10 items in the list. In the case of providing country information, users can more easily type in a country code than choose their country from a long list (**Figure 9.1**).

In general, good form design is a process of simplification and clarification. When designing a Web form, include only the essential elements, and make sure they are clearly described. Use the form element best suited to collecting the necessary information, always from the viewpoint of the user.

Here are some additional suggestions for effective form design:

◆ Use simple language. Clearly communicate what information is being requested.

◆ Provide full details. If a field requires a lengthy description, don't skimp on details to conserve screen space.

◆ Use appropriate language. Do not use "surname" or "family name" if "last name" will be more broadly understood.

◆ Provide examples. When information must be entered in a certain format—such as the date format DD/MM/YY for day, month, year—explain the requirements and provide an example for users to follow. If users enter data in an incorrect format—for example, 3/1/2004 instead of 03/01/04—parse the data into the required format rather than ask users to renter the information.

◆ Mark required fields. Clearly indicate which fields are required for form submission. Make sure required fields are truly necessary to the task.

◆ Follow a logical flow. Follow established conventions for gathering information, such as title, first name, last name, company, street address, city, state/province, and so on. For keyboard-only users, make sure the tab order is the same as the visual order of form elements.

◆ Group related elements. Create sections of elements that relate to the same category, such as personal information, contact information, billing information, and so on.

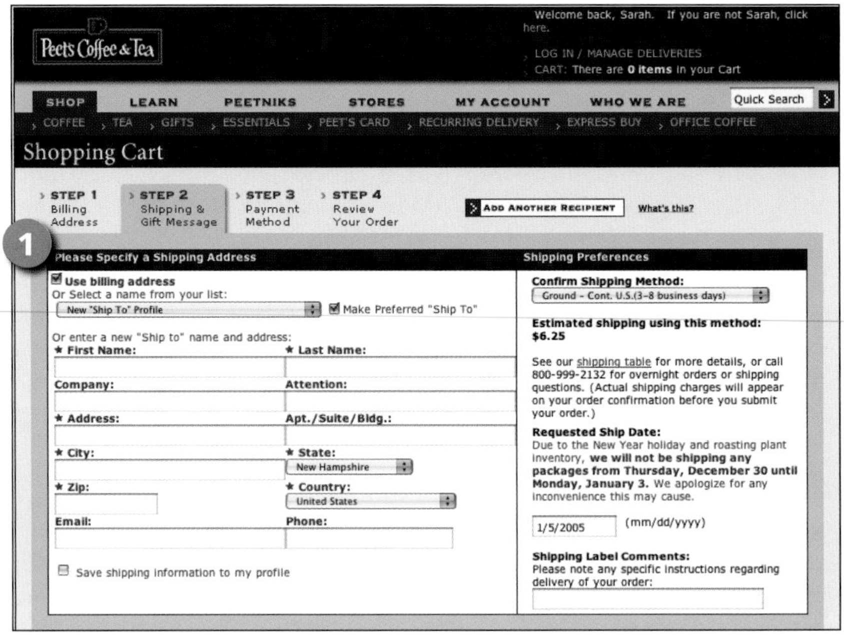

FIGURE 9.2
Good order forms
minimize data entry.
Here, Peet's Coffee
and Tea provides a
"Use billing address"
checkbox (1) that allows
users to enter address
information only once
when the shipping and
billing address are the
same.

- Avoid redundancy. Do not ask users to enter the same information more than once. If the same information might apply in multiple contexts, such as an address for shipping and billing, allow users to indicate that the same information applies (**Figure 9.2**).

In a nutshell. Forms are often difficult to complete because of needless complexity and unclear instructions. Design for clarity and simplicity so users can complete forms successfully.

9.1.2 Provide an alternate to forms

Forms should not be the only way for users to communicate and interact with the individuals, companies, and organizations represented on the Web. A Web site with only forms—no email address, street address, or phone number—is unwelcoming to users who cannot use forms or who prefer to communicate some other way. Forms come with enough technical complexity that some users will inevitably have problems submitting information or ordering items using forms. A phone conversation may be a more effective means of communication than submitting a query over the Web. Web sites that rely solely on forms risk losing users who cannot or choose not to use forms.

Always include alternate methods for making contact, such as a street address, phone number, and email address.

In a nutshell. Web forms may not satisfy the needs of all users. At minimum, provide an email address as an alternate method to communicate and interact with users who cannot or choose not to use forms.

9.2 MARKUP

9.2.1 Label form fields

Labels describe the purpose and function of form elements: for example, the label "month" next to a dropdown menu listing the months of the year, or the label "first name" next to a text input field. Labels are critical because they tell the user what information to provide in the form element.

Designers have other methods to communicate the purpose and function of form fields. Location on the page can offer clues. For example, an unlabeled field in the upper right corner of a Web page is likely to be a search field, while a dropdown menu on the home page is likely to offer quick access to commonly used pages within a site. By following such conventions, designers can save precious screen space by providing form functionality without the necessity of a label. However, when we rely on clues and conventions to communicate the function of such elements, users must decipher the design to use it effectively. Our desire to conserve screen space puts usability at risk because, without an explicit label, users may misinterpret the function of these elements (**Figure 9.3,** *next page*).

A better approach is to label form elements so their purpose is obvious. A label placed near the field it describes lets users know what

FIGURE 9.3

InfoSpace uses default
text (1) to label the
form fields "Type of
Business," "City," and
"State." The label
disappears from "Type
of Business" and "City"
when the fields are
activated by the cursor.

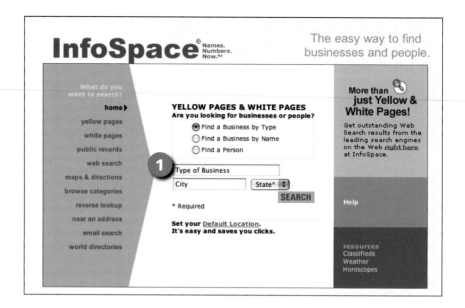

is expected. Users will therefore be more likely to use the element successfully. Nonvisual users do not see the rendered page, but also benefit from proximity: Text that immediately precedes a form field is likely to be its label.

Proximity alone is sometimes insufficient. Nonvisual users often use the tab key to cycle through actionable elements, such as links and form fields. When encountering a form field that is not explicitly labeled, the user knows nothing about the purpose of the field without using other keyboard commands to browse the surrounding text in search of a label. Another possible problem arises when a label does not directly precede its form element in the code. For instance, a disconnect between label and element may occur when forms are embedded within layout tables.

Fortunately, HTML provides the means to explicitly link labels to the form elements that they describe. The purpose and function of form elements is therefore clear regardless of where the elements appear in the code. The LABEL FOR tag associates a form label with its form element using the ID attribute:

```
<label for="search">Search:</label><br />
<input type="text" id="search" name="search" />
```

When labels and elements are linked using the LABEL FOR tag, the function of form fields is clearly identified and can be communicated to nonvisual users.

In a nutshell. Field labels tell users what information to supply in form elements. Label all form fields with self-explanatory labels, and use the LABEL FOR tag to make explicit associations between form elements and their labels.

9.2.2 Associate related form fields

Forms often have different sections for requesting information related to certain categories. For example, an order form may have sections for personal information, shipping information, and billing information. In designing the visual appearance of such a form, we might use headings, borders, color, and proximity to associate the labels, fields, and other form elements that belong within each section, and to differentiate between sections. However, nonvisual users may not be able to discriminate easily between sections without access to these visual cues.

Once again, HTML provides the means to code these relationships so they are available to visual and nonvisual users. Forms can be divided into sections by wrapping the related form elements in the FIELDSET tag and assigning the fieldset a heading using the LEGEND tag. With labeled fieldsets, form controls are grouped into labeled sections that are visually differentiated and can be communicated to the nonvisual user (**Figure 9.4,** *next page*).

In a nutshell. Form elements are often divided into sections based on the type of information that is being requested, such as contact or shipping information. Use the FIELDSET and LEGEND tags to explicitly associate related form elements.

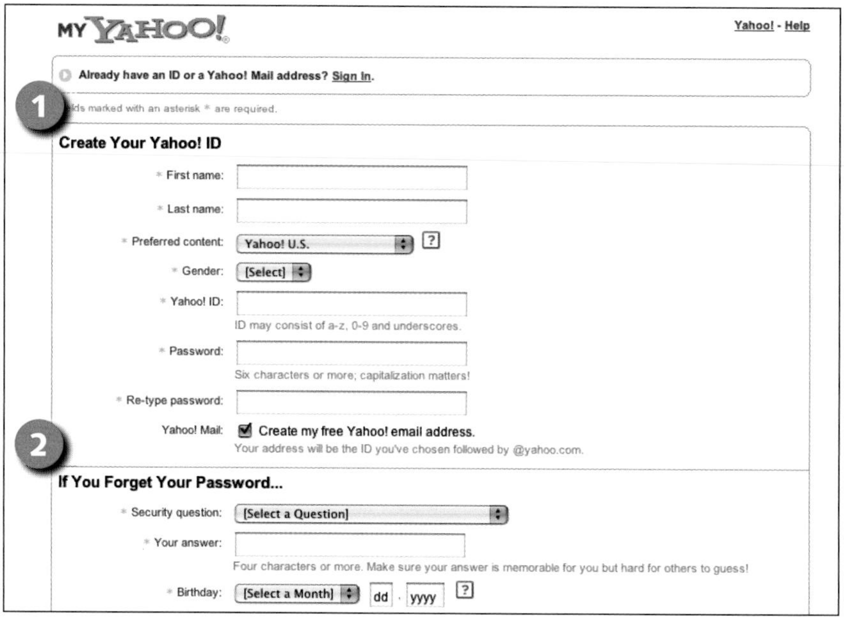

FIGURE 9.4

The My Yahoo! sign-up form is divided into logical sections that are marked by headings (1, 2). The same visual effect could be achieved using the fieldset tag, which would explicitly group the form elements in each section.

9.2.3 Design forms for keyboard accessibility

Many people operate the computer using the keyboard or other input methods that activate keyboard commands. For some people, keyboard accessibility is a preference; for others, a necessity. People who cannot work a pointing device such as a mouse cannot manage point-and-click computer interaction. Interfaces whose controls can only be activated by a pointing device are not accessible to these users. Links and forms are the two primary controls we use to "work" Web sites. For universal usability, these elements must be designed to be operable from the keyboard, in a fashion that is intuitive and meets user expectations.

Keyboard access to forms includes selecting a form element using the tab or arrow key, entering information, perhaps selecting a checkbox, radio button, or menu item, and submitting the form information. People who use a pointing device such as a mouse may choose to point and click to select form elements, but, when designed properly, all these functions are accessible using the keyboard alone.

To design an accessible form it is useful to understand the fundamentals of keyboard access. When using the keyboard, "actionable" elements—such as form elements and links—must first be selected, then activated. For example, pressing the tab or arrow keys moves focus between elements, such as buttons or items on a select menu. Once the desired item has focus, or is selected, pressing the enter key activates the selection. Pressing the enter key on a submit button activates form submission. Specialized software such as screen reader software may provide slightly different controls, but the basic premise of select, then activate, still applies.

Forms can be designed using technologies such as JavaScript and Flash. These add-ons allow designers to have more control over how forms behave and provide more options for interactivity. For example, using JavaScript, a select menu can be coded to activate when a menu item is selected (**Figure 9.5**). This approach may be more economical for mouse users since it requires only one action—selection—to trigger an event, such as loading a page. However, keyboard users will be unable to access such an interface since they need to explicitly select, then activate, to make a menu selection. If selecting a menu item activates it as well, keyboard users will be unable to move past the first menu item.

In a nutshell. Some users navigate and complete forms using the keyboard. Make all form elements operable from the keyboard, and ensure that their behavior is consistent with user expectations.

9.2.4 Apply a logical sequence to form elements

Keyboard users use the tab key to move the cursor through form elements. The tabbing sequence is governed by the order in which elements appear in the code. For visual keyboard users, a logical tab order is convenient, though not essential, since visual users can scan the page to determine which elements are in the form. A form that is out of sequence will be disorienting, but not impossible, to use. On the other hand, usability for nonvisual users suffers when form elements are not in a logical sequence because nonvisual users cannot easily scan the page. Take, for example, a search interface that includes a search field and submit button, followed by radio buttons that allow users to refine their search criteria. Nonvisual users may submit a search without realizing that additional options are available (**Figure 9.6**).

For universal usability, design forms so the elements follow a logical sequence: first name, last name, address, phone number, email address, submit. The information flow is predictable because it mirrors standard practices; anytime a user can successfully predict what comes next, usability is enhanced. Also, be sure that all necessary information appears before the opportunity to submit the form, so users will be less likely to inadvertently submit an incomplete form.

In a nutshell. Keyboard users access Web form elements in the sequence that they appear in the code. Ensure that form elements follow a logical sequence when accessed via the keyboard, and that all essential elements precede the control that submits the form.

FIGURE 9.6
Amazon's advanced
search page displays the
"Search Now" button
after the "Author"
field, even though there
are many more search
options. For better
usability and keyboard
accessibility, the submit
button should appear
after all input fields.

9.2.5 Don't auto-populate form fields with text

Form input fields can be coded to contain text that appears by default in
the text field. Designers often use this technique in place of a field label
to supply information about the purpose of the field. For example, the
default text *search* is common in a search field. Generally this technique
is used to conserve screen real estate: a single search field and submit
button takes up less space than a search label, search field, and submit
button (**Figure 9.7**, *next page*).

When users encounter a field that contains default text, the text
must be removed before they can enter their own text. JavaScript can be
used to automatically remove default text from a text input field. With
this method, when a user clicks or tabs to the field, the default content
disappears and the user can begin typing. Otherwise, the user needs to
delete the text manually before entering information in the field.

Default content causes problems for all users. When JavaScript is
not used or not enabled, the user is responsible for removing the default
text, which may or may not be successful. Designers who use this technique may see *search* listed as one of their site's top search queries, as

FIGURE 9.7

Field labels explain the purpose of a field to visual and nonvisual users. In order to conserve screen space, labels are often left off (1) or supplied using default field text (2), which can cause usability problems. The best approach is to use a text label (3) marked with the LABEL FOR tag to explicitly bind label and field.

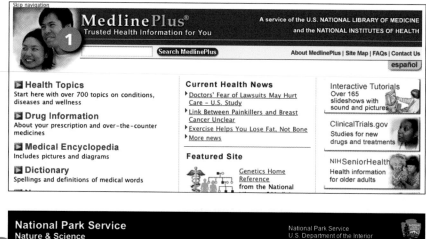

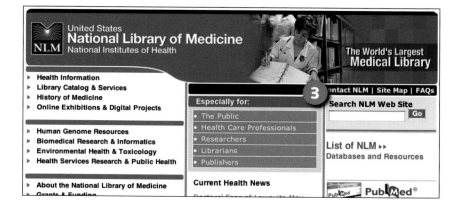

some users may neglect to remove the default text before submitting a search. When JavaScript is used to eliminate the problem by removing the default text, the field loses its label because the default text that serves as field label disappears when the field is activated. This is less of a problem for visual users than for nonvisual users. Visual users can see the field contents and understand its purpose before activating the field. Nonvisual don't "see" the field until it's activated, at which time the label describing its purpose is gone.

The best way, by far, to label form fields is to use a field label, as described above. Properly labeled fields work for all users and do not present usability challenges. Create designs that can accommodate the additional space required for field labels rather than using a workaround, such as default text.

In a nutshell. Using default text to label text input fields creates usability problems for visual and nonvisual users. Use a label rather than default content to indicate the purpose of a text input field.

9.2.6 Use form elements correctly

The basic form elements are text input fields, radio buttons, checkboxes, and select menus. Text input fields are used to collect information that cannot be anticipated by the designer, such as name and address, whereas menu-style elements, such as radio buttons, checkboxes, and select menus, are used for fields where the possible input values can be predicted—gender, title, country, state, and so on. These menu-style form elements can cause usability problems when used incorrectly.

Here are guidelines for designing usable menus:

♦ Use radio buttons and select menus for menus that support one choice among two or more options. (Select menus can support multiple choices. However, this approach is not recommended because of the usability challenges it presents. For fields with more than one possible choice, checkboxes are more usable than multiple-selection menus.)

- Use checkboxes for menus that support multiple choices.
- Use a single checkbox for binary selections, such as yes/no choices, where checked means "yes" and unchecked means "no" (**Figure 9.8**).
- Do not set the default value of a single checkbox to "checked." Otherwise, users may inadvertently say "yes" to receiving an email newsletter or saving an account name and password.
- When appropriate, provide a null or "no response" option for menus and radio buttons. For example, begin a Title menu with "one" or "No title" and then list the possible title choices (Dr., Mrs., Ms., Mr., and so on) or get feedback using radio buttons for Excellent, Good, Poor, No Opinion. Otherwise, users may submit inaccurate information because their accurate or preferred choice is not listed in the menu.

In a nutshell. When used properly, menu fields, such as checkboxes, radio buttons, and select menus, can enhance usability and facilitate data collection. Choose the appropriate menu type, and make item selection an explicit user choice.

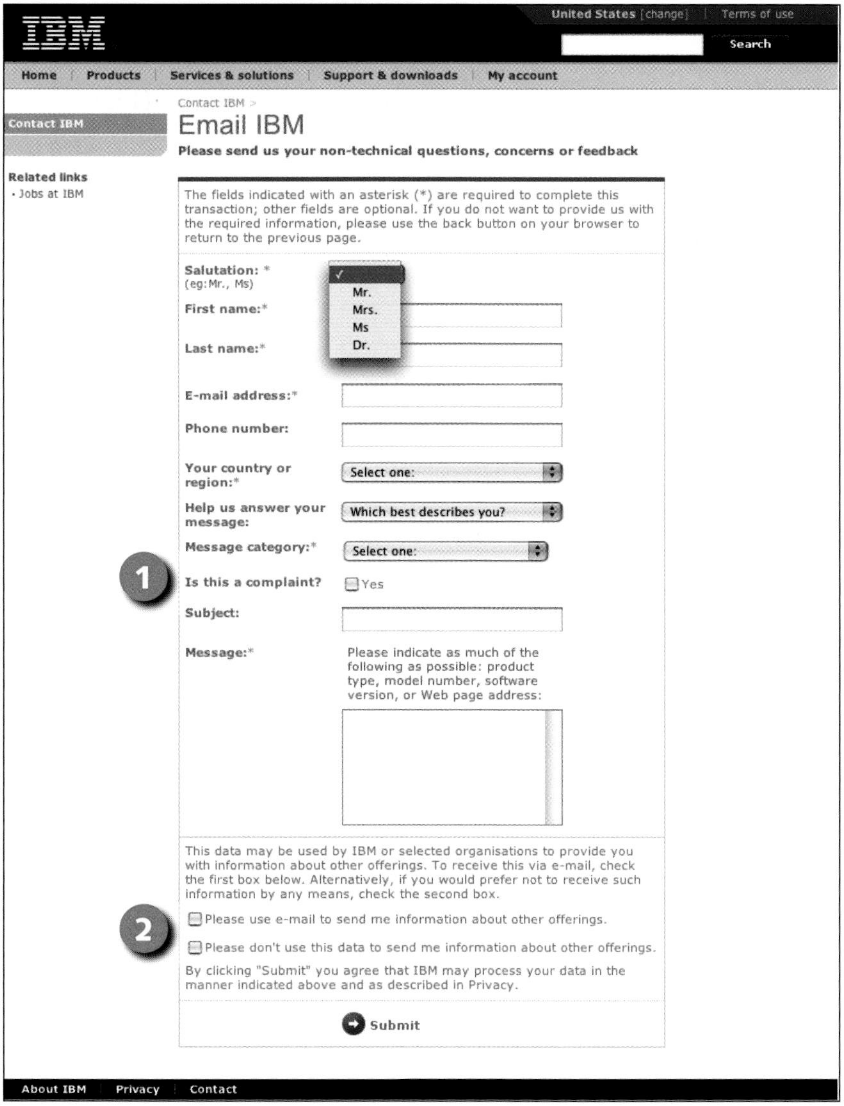

FIGURE 9.8
The IBM Contact form uses a checkbox to pose the question "Is this a complaint?" as a binary choice with the default response of "no" since the checkbox is unchecked (1). However, the question about receiving email about other offerings is presented incorrectly as two checkboxes (2), allowing users to elect both to receive and not receive the information. "Please use e-mail to send me information about other offerings" should be a single checkbox that is unchecked by default.

CHAPTER 10
Links

L INKS ARE TO THE WEB as a steering wheel is to a car: they enable users to navigate their course through hypertext documents. Like a car without a steering wheel, a Web page without links is of little service. When using the Web, we spend much—even most—of our time following links. Therefore, links must be functional and usable.

Links are best displayed as text. Although images can be used for links, they are not flexible, which means that people who need a customized view may not be able to access image links. Additionally, image links without alt-text are virtually useless to nonvisual users because they do not provide descriptive information in a format that is machine-readable (**Figure 10.1**). Given that text is the most accessible form of content, links displayed as text are the most likely to be usable by all.

FIGURE 10.1

Alt-text makes images "visible" to nonvisual users. When sites, such as KidsHealth, do not provide alt-text with their image links, nonvisual users have no way of knowing how to navigate the site.

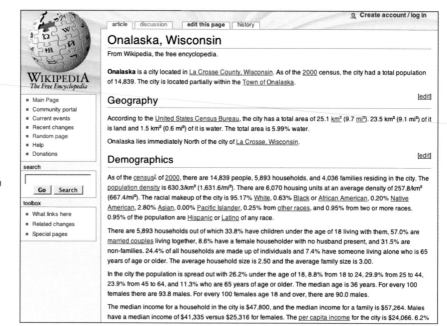

From an editorial perspective, links can be made more accessible and usable when we carefully consider the text we use to describe them. Links that are not descriptive require users to read the surrounding text—or worse, to follow the link to determine its destination. Link text should describe the target of the link, beginning with descriptive keywords to facilitate scanning. For example, "Learn more about <u>reading tea leaves</u>" is easier to scan than "<u>Learn more about reading tea leaves</u>."

From a design perspective, links must be visually differentiated from other page elements so that users can identify them. Inline text links should be colored and underlined. Navigation links should be set off by their design and location—for example, by marking them with borders or tabs and placing them along the top or left column of the page. In terms of color, visited links should be colored differently from regular links so that users know which pages they have already visited. Links to the current page should be identified using color or some other visible highlight that tells the user "You are here" (**Figure 10.2**).

FIGURE 10.3
Audible.com uses a tab
interface to provide
access to the main
sections of the site. The
tabs are designed using
images, which ensures
a stable design even
with different text sizes
and window widths.
However, users who
need a customized view
cannot modify these
essential links.

10.1 BASIC PRINCIPLES

10.1.1 Use text for links

Using the Web is largely a process of moving from page to page. Links
are the controls that we use to power and control that process. Without
access to links, our Web use is significantly compromised. Links should
therefore be presented as text in order to be universally usable.

Web pages often incorporate navigation links into an overall page
design—for example, into a page header that includes other elements
such a logo or photograph. Sometimes navigation links and design elements are tightly integrated, as in the common navigation interface that
provides links to different sections through tabs (**Figure 10.3**). When
navigation is tied tightly to other design elements, the overall design is
generally less amenable to change. Integrated designs that contain links
and other design elements may not adapt gracefully to enlarged type, for
example, or different window widths.

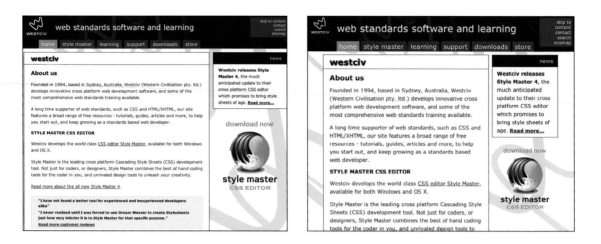

FIGURE 10.4

Westciv provides tab
navigation on its Web
site using list markup
and CSS styling. Since
the tabs are text-based,
they adapt to user
modification without
compromising the
integrity of the design.

One way to ensure design integrity is to use images for navigation links. Tab navigation that is presented as an image will not resize to accommodate different text settings, or wrap to adapt to different window widths. Image-based navigation also allows for typographic effects and treatments, such as specialized fonts and drop-shadows.

Images can be problematic for some users. Navigation presented as images cannot be modified, so users who need large type or certain color combinations may not be able to access navigation links when they are provided as images. Nonvisual users cannot access information presented in image format unless alt-text is provided. Each image link must have descriptive alt-text for image-based navigation to be accessible to nonvisual users.

On the other hand, links that are presented in text format can be accessed and customized as needed—enlarged, recolored, read by software. Text downloads much more quickly than images, which means that navigation options are readily available, even over a slow modem connection. Unlike images, text is not resolution-dependent, which means that it displays more consistently across devices. Given that links are the most basic requirement for functioning Web pages, text is undoubtedly the most effective medium for providing universal access to links.

Text-based navigation need not be visually bereft. A list of links can be styled most gracefully using css, which provides options for text formatting, coloring, and borders. Each new version of css introduces additional text formatting properties. When text and css are used instead of images to design navigation, pages are attractive and usable, adapting gracefully to user modifications, such as enlarged type (**Figure 10.4**).

In a nutshell. Access to links is essential for Web usability. Use text for links, and style them using style sheets.

10.1.2 Use descriptive link text

When we arrive at a Web page, our first task is often to skim the page for links. Visually, text links are easy to identify since they are normally colored and underlined, and so stand out from the other information on the page. Nonvisual users can easily identify links since links are tagged and therefore identifiable by software—for instance, search engine software scans pages for links and follows them to create an index of Web pages, and screen reader software offers a "links list" with the available links on the page.

For effective skimming, both visual and nonvisual users benefit from link text that can stand on its own without the surrounding context of the page. Good link text provides a clear description of the page that will load when following a link. With good link text, users can skim links and make quick, informed decisions about the path to take to accomplish their task. With bad link text, users cannot ascertain the target of the link from the link text alone. Common examples of bad link text are the "click here" and "more" links that proliferate on the Web. This type of link text offers no explanation; it requires that users expand their focus to the surrounding context or follow the link to discover its destination. Nondescriptive link text slows progress and often sends users down the wrong path.

When skimming links, the first words in the link text are the ones most likely to grab the user's attention. Link text that begins with keywords is easier to skim efficiently and works better with software features such as

FIGURE 10.5

Nondescriptive links, such as the "More info..." links on the Shutterfly details page, require users to expand their focus to determine the target of the link. They also undermine features such as the Links List shown here.

link lists that provide an alphabetized list of links on a page. When links begin with nondescriptive words—such as "<u>All about bear hibernation</u>" or "<u>Learn more about squirrel-proof birdhouses</u>"—skimming is slowed and the alphabetized links list is not useful. A better approach is to use only the keywords for link text: "All about <u>bear hibernation</u>" and "Learn more about <u>squirrel-proof birdhouses</u>" (**Figure 10.5**).

In a nutshell. Descriptive link text makes navigation easier and more efficient because descriptive links are easier to skim and allow users to make informed choices. Make link text clear and self-explanatory to support quick and effective navigation.

10.2.1 Underline links that are not otherwise identifiable as links

Links are the primary means for navigating the Web. To make use of links, users must be able to identify them. Browser software addresses this requirement by coloring and underlining links so they stand out from other page elements. This method has built-in redundancy—coloring and underlining—so that people who cannot access color information will still be able to identify links.

In design terms, underlining is a typographical *faux pas* carried over from the days of the typewriter. Before computers, people wrote by hand or on a typewriter, where italic and bold formatting are not readily available. In these mediums, underlining is a convention used to indicate a book title, a section heading, and other forms of emphasis. With the advent of computers and word-processing, bold and italic formatting is just a click away, though some people continue to use underlining for emphasis. (On the Web, underlining should never be used for typographic emphasis. Since Web links are underlined, underlined text that is *not* a link will confuse users.)

The reason underlines are seen as a typographic blemish is that they draw the eye and intersect with letterforms in a way that is ungainly in comparison with other methods of emphasis. Web designers concerned about typographic integrity have long objected to link underlines but, before css, had little control over their display.

Link underlining is a user-defined setting; users can choose whether or not to underline links via browser preferences. However, css allows Web designers to remove link underlines, and this style attribute takes precedence over user preferences. If a designer uses css to remove link underlines, users who depend on underlines to identify links have only one option: to tell their browser not to load author-defined styles.

For Web pages to be universally usable, links must be identifiable in a way that is accessible with or without color information. Underlining is the most standard method, but there are other methods for marking links. Placement on the page—such as in button bars and navigation

FIGURE 10.6

The site navigation links
on the Hubble site are
not underlined or colored
because their placement
and visual formatting
identify them as links.
However, links within the
body text are underlined
and colored.

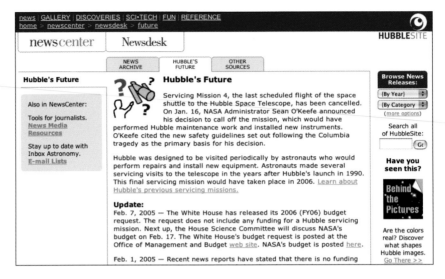

columns—or visual attributes—such as bevels, outlines, or icons—can
be used in place of underlines to denote links as long as the links are
clearly identifiable. However, do not remove underlining from links that
have no other identifier, such as links within body text (**Figure 10.6**).

In a nutshell. Some users cannot distinguish colors and rely on other
visual cues to identify links. Do not rely on color alone to identify links;
use underlines or other visual indicators—such as borders or buttons—
to mark links.

10.2.2 Differentiate visited and unvisited links

Browsers keep track of Web use by saving identifying information about
the pages that have been visited. This stored "history" is what enables
users to use the History menu to backtrack to pages they visited days
ago, or to use the back button to retrace their most recent steps. The
history also allows the browser to identify links on a page that have
already been visited.

When navigating a body of information as vast as the Web, it
becomes extremely important to recognize the pages that have already

FIGURE 10.7
The IBM Accessibility
Center uses a less-
saturated version of the
standard blue and purple
link colors to clearly mark
visited and unvisited
links.

been visited. Very often Web use is a quest for information—a phone number, a name, a price—and without some means to identify the places they have already looked, the users' route can quickly become circuitous. When visited and unvisited links are not differentiated, the only way to determine whether a page has been visited may be to visit it again (and again, and again). When links are visually differentiated, users can proceed more efficiently by avoiding pages that did not prove fruitful.

The standard browser default is to color unvisited links blue and visited links purple. This combination is the most universal and will be generally recognizable, even with some variation in saturation and brightness (perhaps slate blue and violet). However, since this combination is so universal, designers should avoid using its opposite: purple text for unvisited links and blue text for visited. Another approach is to use a saturated color for unvisited links and a less bright, less saturated version of the same color for visited links (such as slate blue for unvisited links, dark slate blue for visited links) (**Figure 10.7**).

FIGURE 10.8
Nutrition.gov uses
breadcrumb navigation
marked by a "You are
here" heading to inform
users where they are in
the site and to provide
a means to navigate
back through the site
hierarchy.

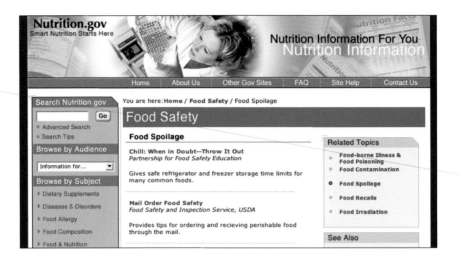

In a nutshell. The ability to distinguish between visited and unvisited links helps keep users from revisiting pages that did not prove successful. Differentiate unvisited and visited links so that users can identify the pages that they have already visited.

10.2.3 Provide "you are here" orientation cues

Orientation is the first stage in wayfinding—the process of using information devices such as maps and signs to *find the way* to a destination. Used on maps in zoos, malls, museums, parks, and so on, the "you are here" indicator orients users as to where they are in the overall context. A map without orientation cues requires that users attempt to identify their location on a map by looking for landmarks.

For Web users, disorientation is a common condition. Simply following a few link paths can cause users to lose track of their location within the overall organization of a site. Designers can help users stay on track by using wayfinding orientation cues to tell users where they are in the overall context of the site.

If we think of navigation as the map of a site, the "you are here" indicator can be easily incorporated into navigation design. One method for providing navigation and orientation is to use what are commonly

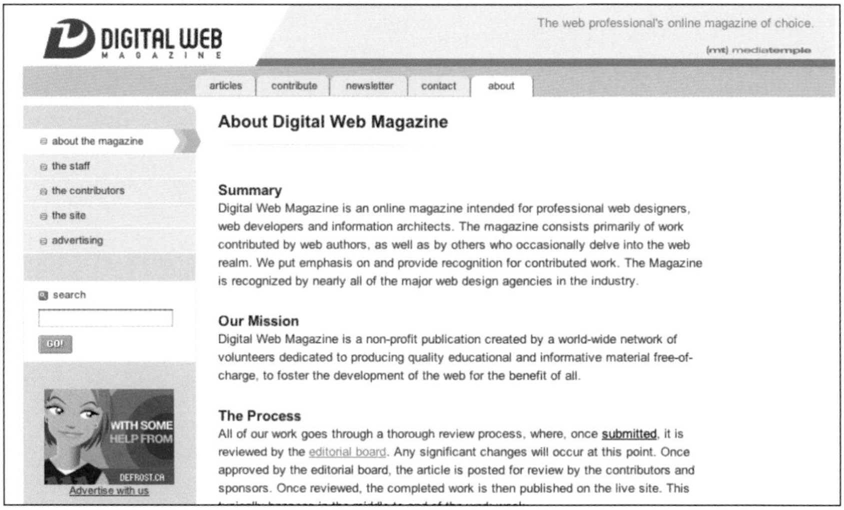

FIGURE 10.9
Digital Web Magazine displays a prominent "You are here" indicator in the site's section navigation links. A stylized green arrow points from the navigation link to the page content area.

referred to as "breadcrumb" navigation links. Breadcrumbs have the benefit of showing the current page as well as where the page lies in the overall site hierarchy (**Figure 10.8**). Another method is to provide a visual marker that makes the current page link stand out from the other navigation links. The link may be a different color, different weight, or different background color. The link may be disabled so users won't click on a link to the current page. Often a marker is added next to the link to visually tell users "you are here" (**Figure 10.9**).

If the "you are here" marker is achieved visually—through color or typographic emphasis—non-visual users will not have access to orientation information. For nonvisual users to access orientation information, the indicator must be somehow represented in the code. A breadcrumb path, preceded by a "you are here" heading, conveys orientation information both visually and in the code. Another option is to combine a visible marker with the alt-text "current page" into the current page link.

In a nutshell. Users can easily become disoriented when navigating the Web. Use orientation cues—such as an arrow marker next to the current page link—to identify the current page.

10.2.4 Use alt-text for image links

When using images as links, alt-text becomes the link text for nonvisual users. When software encounters an image that is used as a link, it cannot "read" the image of, for example, the word *Home* or *Products* or *Support*. If descriptive text is provided in the image tag (alt="Home", alt="Products", alt="Support"), then software can use the alt-text to describe the link to the user. If no alt-text is provided, software has little information to go on. Some software will read the target of the link, which might suffice if the file names are descriptive: "home.html", "products.html", "support.html". However, many file names are not readily identifiable; a products page on large-scale site might be one of many, with a file name like "products/electronic/fall2004/14359035.asp".

Generally, text is the best way to provide the essential functionality of links. Text is flexible and machine-friendly; as such, it is the most universally accessible and usable format for providing basic navigation control to all users. That said, when using images as links, be sure to provide alt-text in the image tag using a self-explanatory link label. With image maps, provide alt-text for each area of the map. Without alternative text for image links, people who cannot access images may be unable to navigate the site (**Figure 10.10**).

In a nutshell. Without alt-text, image-based navigation is virtually inaccessible to nonvisual users. Provide descriptive alternate text for image links, including links in image maps, for users who cannot access images.

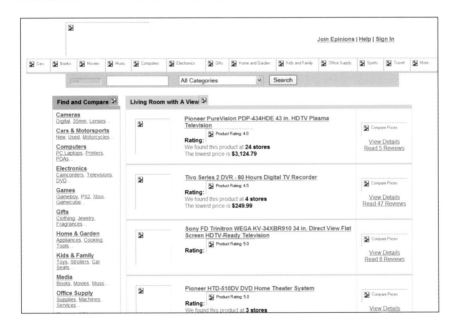

FIGURE 10.10
Epinions provides
equivalent alt-text for
its image-based site
navigation links. The
alternate text makes the
site navigation accessible
to nonvisual users.

CHAPTER 11

Color

O N THE WEB, COLOR IS A VISUAL DESIGN ELEMENT that is
truly without cost. Like images, designers can use colors freely
and easily; unlike images, users do not pay the price because color settings do not increase page load or rendering times. Color is a powerful
tool for visual design; it can be used to set tone, draw attention, convey
information, differentiate elements, and more.

However, color can impair usability. Legibility suffers when the contrast between text and background is insufficient. When text is set with
low contrast, character shapes are difficult to distinguish, which makes
reading difficult and tiring. For best legibility, complementary elements
such as text and background should use complementary colors.

Nonvisual users cannot see color, and some visual users cannot distinguish certain colors or are using technology that does not display
color. When color is used to communicate information—for example, to
identify required fields or to emphasize important text—such users may
not be able to access the information. For universal usability, pages must
be usable without color.

Some people have viewing requirements for colors, such as a high-
contrast view (a black background with white or yellow text). The best
way to design for specialized needs is to define color settings so users
who have special color needs can apply their own settings.

11.1 BASIC PRINCIPLES

11.1.1 Select contrasting colors for greatest legibility
Legibility is greatly affected by the perceived contrast between text and
background. With low-contrast typography, reading is difficult since

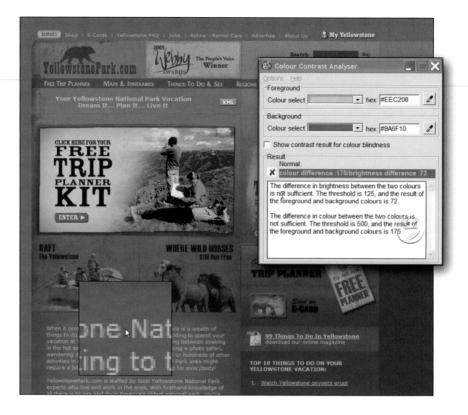

readers must work to distinguish letterforms. A document set with pink text on a red background would be tiring, if not impossible, to read.

Color perception is affected by many factors, including physiological factors such as aging and color-blindness and environment factors such as display settings and room lighting. When designing elements that require clarity and definition—such as text—choose colors for perceptibility and legibility above all other considerations to avoid using color combinations that make it difficult for users to distinguish foreground from background (**Figure 11.1**).

Color differentiation is most influenced by contrast in brightness, or light-dark contrast. Brightness is the amount of white that is present in a color. Pairing black with white provides the greatest brightness

Brightness contrast increases legibility

Brightness contrast increases legibility

Brightness contrast increases legibility

Brightness contrast increases legibility

Brightness contrast increases legibility

Complementary colors are most effective

Complementary colors are most effective

Adjacent colors are less effective

Adjacent colors are less effective

FIGURE 11.2
Text is most legible when foreground and background colors differ in brightness. As brightness contrast diminishes, so does legibility. Hue also affects color differentiation. Complementary colors produce more contrast than colors that are adjacent on the color wheel.

contrast since white has a 100% brightness value, whereas black has a brightness value of 0%. Legibility is greatest when the degree of brightness contrast between text and background is high (**Figure 11.2**).

Hue is also a factor in color differentiation. Greatest contrast is achieved by using complementary hues—that is, colors that are on opposing sides of the color circle—and by combining dark colors from the bottom half of the color circle with light colors from the upper half of the circle (Figure 11.2).

In a nutshell. Readability suffers when there is insufficient contrast between text and background. Maximize legibility by using color combinations that contrast in brightness (such as black and white) and hue (such as purple and yellow).

11.1.2 Don't use color alone to convey meaning

When color is used to enhance or enliven the visual display of a page, people who cannot access color will not necessarily suffer from reduced usability. They will still be able to access the materials on the site and to operate the site functions. However, when color is an integral part of the user interface, people who cannot access color may encounter difficulties. When color is used to convey information or to provide direction—as an indicator, to draw attention to interface elements or important text, and to provide status information—nonvisual users as well as some visual users will be affected.

For example, required form fields are commonly identified using red text for the field label (**Figure 11.3**). Nonvisual users will not be able to identify required fields because the software reads the content of the page, not its visual characteristics. Visual users who cannot distinguish the color red will therefore not be able to identify required fields. Other examples include alert text displayed as red text, and colored buttons.

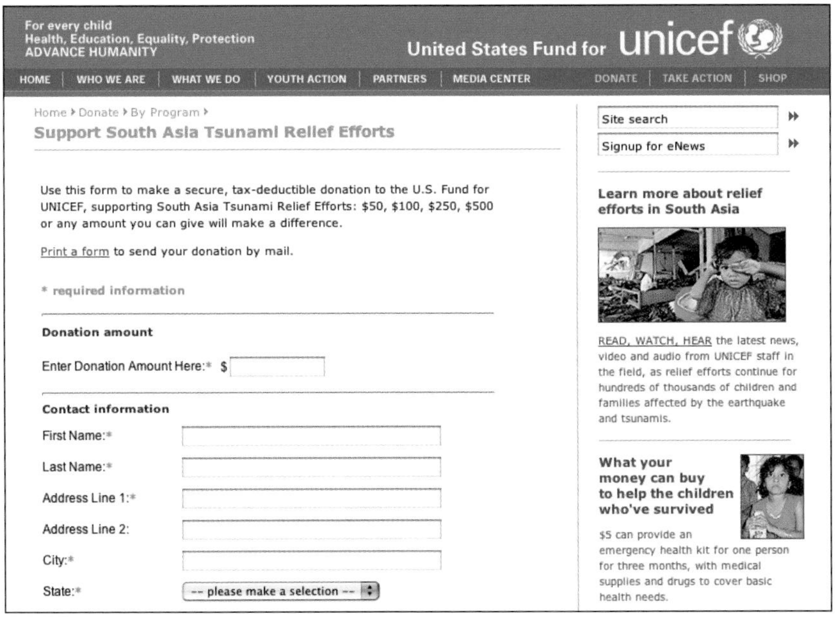

FIGURE 11.4
UNICEF uses a colored asterisk to identify required fields. The color makes the fields easy to identify for users who access color, and the asterisk can be identified and understood by all users.

As with other potential obstacles, the solution is not to eschew color. Color is an extremely effective method for creating emphasis and providing feedback—two essential aspects of a user interface. The solution is to provide redundant emphasis and feedback using other, accessible methods.

Links are a good model for this type of redundancy. On the Web, links have built-in visual attributes: color and underlines. Users who can see color can identify links by looking for colored text. Users who cannot distinguish colors can identify links by looking for underlined text. Because links are machine-readable, nonvisual users also have a means for identifying links. Screen readers distinguish links from other text by reading them using a different voice. Screen reader users can cycle through the links on a page using the tab key, access a list of links, and ask software to read only links. Software's ability to recognize links is what allows search engines to rank pages based on link frequency.

When using color to emphasize elements that do not have built-in redundancy, we need to take into account nonvisual users and visual users who cannot access color. The best way to design for these users is to provide emphasis using text as well as color. For example, instead of using color to identify required form fields, use color and an asterisk, and advise users that "Required fields are red and marked with an asterisk" (**Figure 11.4**, *previous page*). Instead of using color to highlight alert text, use color and text, such as "ALERT! Your username and password are incorrect." Rather than ask users to "Click the red button to continue," instruct users to "Click the Submit button to continue."

In a nutshell. Some users cannot see color, while others have difficulties distinguishing certain colors. When using color to convey information, reinforce color with text so people who cannot access color can access the information.

11.2 MARKUP

11.2.1 Allow users to override color settings

To design a Web page, we must make decisions about the visual characteristics of the page. In terms of color, we make decisions about page color, text color, the color of page elements and areas, link colors, button colors, and more.

In a fixed medium, a user who has difficulties with a document's chosen colors has little opportunity to modify those characteristics. If the designated colors make it difficult to read the document, or if other color combinations are needed for reading, the user may have difficulty accessing the content of the document.

On the Web, color settings are flexible and can be user-defined. When users encounter a document with colors that get in the way of usability, they can override the color settings by changing browser settings or by applying a custom style sheet.

When designing color, use methods that can be overridden by the user. Colors set in style sheets are easily customized using user style

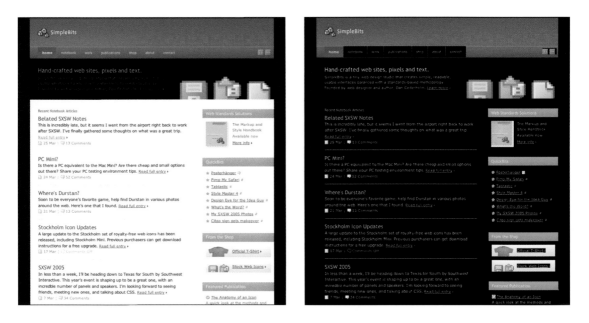

sheets. Colors set on the page are less flexible. For example, when colors are defined in the HTML code, users cannot selectively override color settings. They have no choice but to override all color settings and display the page using the browser-defined color settings.

Colors in graphics cannot be customized. If users have difficulty with the colors in an image, they have no way to remedy the display so as to access the content. When essential elements such as headings and links are presented as images, users who need custom colors may be unable to use the site. On the other hand, when color is applied using HTML and styles, designers have a way to define, and users to customize, color in the user interface (**Figure 11.5**).

In a nutshell. Users may need to apply customized color settings to access Web content. Use styles to define colors so users can easily override color settings. Avoid using images, which cannot be customized, for essential page content.

FIGURE 11.5

When colors are specified in style sheets, users who need certain colors can override the author-defined styles and apply their own custom color settings. SimpleBits has a flexible design that can accommodate this level of customization.

Audio and Video

AUDIO AND VIDEO SHARE the same fundamental challenge as all nontext content: Some users will be unable to access the information since it's available through only one sense: either vision or hearing. Audio can only be heard; video can only be seen. On the other hand, text is versatile because—thanks to text-to-speech technology—it can be both seen *and* heard. Consequently, the primary task of delivering accessible media is to provide a text equivalent for both visual and audible components.

Audio and video also present technical challenges. The technical requirements for network delivery of them are high—too high for some users. Users with slow Internet access may not be able to receive the large amount of data required for media. Furthermore, because digital media files are so large, Web video and audio are by necessity greatly compressed and require a fast computer processor to decompress and play. Older computers may not have the cycles needed to play media files, and some devices, such as PDAs and cell phones, may not support media playback. Finally, support for media formats is not built into browser software, which means users must install special software for playback. Users who cannot access media for technical reasons benefit from text equivalents.

For those who can access audio and video, playback must be accessible and consistent with user expectations. Users must be in control of media elements, making decisions about when to load media, when to play, and so on. For users who rely on keyboard access, media controls—play, pause, and volume—must be accessible from the keyboard.

FIGURE 12.1

The White House site contains an extensive collection of speech transcripts, some with accompanying audio files and some with video. When spoken information is presented with a transcript, users can access the information by listening, reading, or both.

12.1 BASIC PRINCIPLES

12.1.1 Provide text for audio content

Audible content is inaccessible to users who are deaf or hard of hearing. Other users may be unable to access audio for environmental reasons—for example, because they are accessing the Web in a public space, or using a device such as a handheld or cell phone that does not support audio output. To make audio accessible, the equivalent content must be available as text.

Audio content comes in various forms—from music to sound to spoken narration and dialogue. While words cannot *represent* music or sound, words can *describe* them. Captions, for example, often describe sounds such as glass breaking or a car door slamming. On the other hand, spoken audio can be effectively represented as text. For example, a text transcript of a lecture or speech has the equivalent information contained in the audio presentation. When providing access to spoken audio, provide a text version along with the audio file. With both the audio file and

transcript readily available, users can choose to read, listen, or both (**Figure 12.1**).

When audio is part of a video presentation, a text transcript alone will not suffice. Users who cannot hear need access to the information contained in the audio while viewing the video. In this case, synchronize the text with the video by using captions (**Figure 12.2**).

When providing access to audio via synchronized captions, a separate page containing the text transcript may be useful to users who cannot access the video—for example, because they do not have the correct plugin or are connecting to the Internet using a slow modem. Also, some users may prefer to access the transcript alone, perhaps for printing and review. Additionally, a text transcript improves search engine indexing.

In a nutshell. Some users cannot access audio. Supply a text transcript of audio content; when audio is part of video, also synchronize the transcript as captions.

FIGURE 12.2

The Nova site is exemplary in providing captioned videos. Here, users can choose to view the video with or without captions. Users can also access the audio portion of the video via a text transcript.

12.1.2 Provide descriptions for video content

Video presents the same access challenge as images: how to make visual information accessible to nonvisual users. As with images, the solution is to supply an alternate description. The difficulty in describing video is that there are many, many images to describe. If one picture is worth a thousand words, how many words are needed to describe a 3-minute video!

Fortunately, video usually comes with an audio track that provides information about what is happening on screen. Indeed, for much video, listening alone is likely to provide more information than watching without audio. In addition, descriptions can be used to "fill in the blanks," providing pertinent information contained in the video for nonvisual users. Descriptions are supplied during the pauses in the audio portion of a video, either through recorded audio or text that can be read by software. Accessible video contains synchronized captions for nonhearing users and synchronized descriptions for nonvisual users (**Figure 12.3**).

As with text transcripts for audio, providing descriptions separate from the video is a good way to provide the information to users who cannot access the video. A single text file containing both the video descriptions and the audio transcript will provide users who cannot access the video much of the necessary information (Figure 12.3).

In a nutshell. Some users cannot access video. Use synchronized descriptions to provide pertinent details about video, along with a separate file containing text descriptions and the audio transcript for users who cannot access video files.

12.1.3 Provide alternate formats for media-based content

Access to audio and video content places significant demands on the user. First, users must be able to see and hear. From a technology standpoint, digital media require much more data than text or images. Users with slow Internet access will have difficultly downloading all the bits associated with media files. Additionally, digital media must be greatly compressed to make files small enough for network delivery. Users with

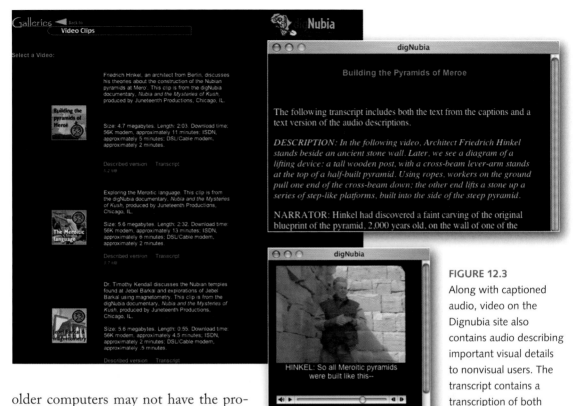

Galleries ◀ Back to
Video Clips

Select a Video:

Building the
pyramids of
Meroe

Friedrich Hinkel, an architect from Berlin, discusses his theories about the construction of the Nubian pyramids at Meroï. This clip is from the digNubia documentary, *Nubia and the Mysteries of Kush*, produced by Juneteenth Productions, Chicago, IL.

Size: 4.7 megabytes. Length: 2:03. Download time: 56K modem, approximately 11 minutes; ISDN, approximately 5 minutes; DSL/Cable modem, approximately 2 minutes.

Described version   Transcript
6.2 MB

The Meroitic
language

Exploring the Meroitic language. This clip is from the digNubia documentary, *Nubia and the Mysteries of Kush*, produced by Juneteenth Productions, Chicago, IL.

Size: 5.6 megabytes. Length: 2:32. Download time: 56K modem, approximately 13 minutes; ISDN, approximately 6 minutes; DSL/Cable modem, approximately 2 minutes.

Described version   Transcript
5.7 MB

Jebel Barkal &
magnetometry

Dr. Timothy Kendall discusses the Nubian temples found at Jebel Barkal and explorations of Jebel Barkal using magnetometry. This clip is from the digNubia documentary, *Nubia and the Mysteries of Kush*, produced by Juneteenth Productions, Chicago, IL.

Size: 5.6 megabytes. Length: 0:55. Download time: 56K modem, approximately 4.5 minutes; ISDN, approximately 2 minutes; DSL/Cable modem, approximately .5 minutes.

Described version   Transcript

Nubia

digNubia

Building the Pyramids of Meroe

The following transcript includes both the text from the captions and a text version of the audio descriptions.

DESCRIPTION: In the following video, Architect Friedrich Hinkel stands beside an ancient stone wall. Later, we see a diagram of a lifting device: a tall wooden post, with a cross-beam lever-arm stands at the top of a half-built pyramid. Using ropes, workers on the ground pull one end of the cross-beam down; the other end lifts a stone up a series of step-like platforms, built into the side of the steep pyramid.

NARRATOR: Hinkel had discovered a faint carving of the original blueprint of the pyramid, 2,000 years old, on the wall of one of the

digNubia

HINKEL: So all Meroitic pyramids
were built like this--

Friedrich Hinkel, an architect from Berlin, discusses his theories about the construction of the Nubian pyramids at Meroï. This clip is from the digNubia documentary, *Nubia and the Mysteries of Kush*, produced by Juneteenth Productions, Chicago, IL.

FIGURE 12.3
Along with captioned audio, video on the Dignubia site also contains audio describing important visual details to nonvisual users. The transcript contains a transcription of both the audio and the audio descriptions.

older computers may not have the processor power needed for decompression and playback. Moreover, audio and video come in different formats, all of which require a plugin for access. Whenever access to content requires a special software installation, universal usability is compromised, because many factors can interfere with a successful installation.

As discussed throughout this book, the best format for providing universal access to content is text. For nontext formats—such as images, audio, and video—alternate access can be provided using text. A transcript and captions can provide access for users who cannot hear the audio. A description of the video content can provide access to users

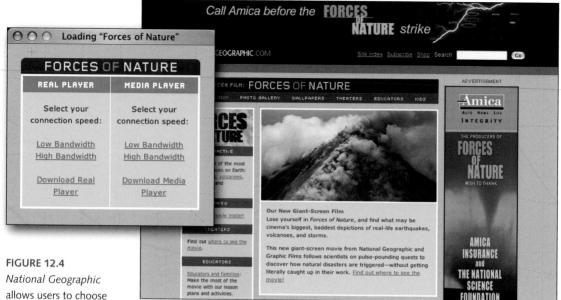

FIGURE 12.4

National Geographic allows users to choose between media formats—Real Player and Media Player—and also between low- and high-bandwidth versions.

who cannot see the video. In addition, text can provide access to users stymied by technical limitations. A page containing the text transcript and relevant still frames is a useful and reliable alternative to a video presentation since access does not require special software or a high-speed network connection.

When providing video and audio, allow users to choose from low, medium, and high bandwidth versions of the media file—particularly when offering video, which is far more bandwidth-intensive than audio. Also consider providing the content in different formats, such as QuickTime, Real, or MPEG-4, and allow users to choose their preferred format (**Figure 12.4**).

In a nutshell. Many factors can impede access to media, including physical or technical limitations. When providing content using audio and video, supply alternatives so users can choose the version that best suits their needs and preferences.

12.1.4 Make media keyboard accessible

For universal usability, all actionable elements on a Web page must be accessible from the keyboard. Keyboard accessibility ensures that pages are operable for nonvisual users and for visual users who cannot or prefer not to use a pointing device, such as a mouse. Media elements normally have elements of interaction. At minimum, media playback is controllable though play and pause buttons. Some media formats allow designers to build in extensive interactivity. For example, QuickTime provides an extensive set of tools for adding interactivity to a media presentation.

In order to support keyboard access, all interactivity must support the basic select and activate functions required for keyboard access. Keyboard users select elements by using the tab or arrow keys and, when desired, click the enter key to activate the element and trigger its associated function. For media playback, keyboard users must have the ability to select and then activate the play and pause buttons. Volume control

FIGURE 12.5

In general, player applications, such as QuickTime Player, are more fully featured than the simple controller bar that displays with media that is embedded on a Web page, and are easier to control from the keyboard.

is another important playback function; keyboard users must be able to select the volume control and adjust the volume using the arrow keys.

Support for keyboard control varies across browsers and media formats. The controls offered with embedded media—that is, audio or video that is embedded within a Web page—may be less accessible than those offered by the media player software. When offering access to embedded media content, consider also offering the option to play the media file in the corresponding media player as the player may have better keyboard support (**Figure 12.5,** *previous page*).

In a nutshell. Some users navigate the Web using the keyboard. Make sure media controls—such as play and pause—respond to keyboard commands, so users who rely on keyboard navigation can control media playback.

12.1.5 Allow users to control media playback

User control is an important aspect of universal usability. Users must be able to control their environment and to make decisions about what happens on a Web page, and when. This holds true for audio and video content. Given the demands that these elements place on users, audio and video should not appear within the content of a standard Web page. Loading an audio or video file should happen only when the user elects to access the file by clicking on a link. As discussed above, access to video and audio should come with multiple options so users can choose the size and format that best suit their needs.

In addition to controlling when to load media files, users must be in control of media playback. Web pages containing audio and video that is set to play automatically can cause usability problems. For example, some Web pages contain background music that plays automatically when the page is loaded. Imagine accessing a page with background music in a public setting, such as the library, or trying to make sense of it using a screen reader. Without a way to control playback—to pause or control the volume setting—users may be forced to leave the page to regain control of their environment. As with the choice to load media

elements, the choice to play audio or video should always be user-driven. Present media elements with playback controls (**Figure 12.6**). Do not automatically play media; instead, wait for the user to activate the play button.

In a nutshell. Users should decide when to access media. Make loading and playback of media an explicit user choice, and provide controls for playing, pausing, and controlling volume.

FIGURE 12.6
Media must always display with controls that allow users to control media playback. Here, the Real interface used on the *POV* site allows users to control playback, volume, and toggle captions display.

Interactivity

T HE WEB IS BOTH a hypertext system we navigate to find information and a software application we use to accomplish tasks. As a
hypertext system, the Web does an adequate job, with enough built-in
functionality to allow for describing and connecting documents and for
providing document access. As a software application, the Web is less
well equipped.

The Web is a client–server application that does not support page-
level interactivity. Web interactions are based on a dialog between the
Web browser (client) and the Web server (server). The browser requests
a page; the server delivers it. Once the page is delivered, the dialog is
suspended until the browser makes another page request. In the Web
environment, the only way a user can interact with a page is by clicking
on a link or submitting a Web form, which prompts the browser to
reopen its dialog with the server. In fact, links and forms are the Web's
only native modes of interactivity. Links allow users to navigate within
and among documents; forms collect information from users. As such,
the Web cannot provide the level of interactivity that we have come to
expect from desktop and CD-ROM applications.

Some sites use scripts, Java applets, ActiveX, and plugins (such as
Flash or QuickTime) to provide a higher degree of interactivity than
can be provided using standard Web structures. Unfortunately, equitable
and universal access is difficult to provide when essential site content is
designed using nonstandard formats.

Many factors can get in the way of access to nonstandard content.
Users can opt out of nonstandard formats by choosing not to load
required plugins or by disabling Java and JavaScript. Some users may
encounter difficulties downloading and installing plugins. Some system

FIGURE 13.1

Many sites use add-on technologies such as JavaScript to offer interactive features such as this calendar (1) on the Iberia site. These features often add complexity and hinder accessibility rather than improve usability.

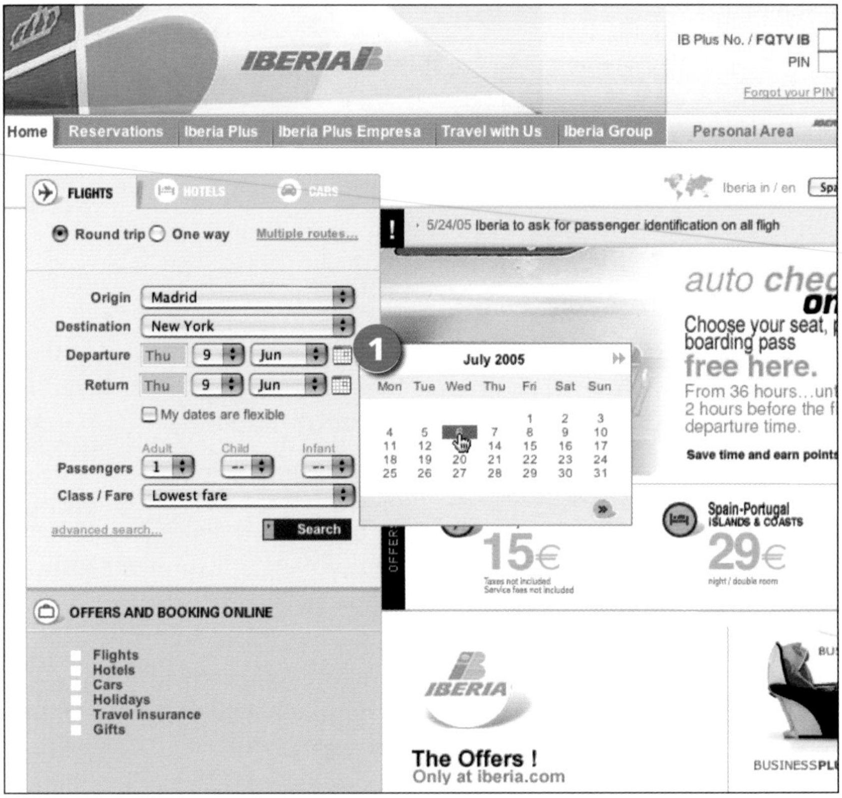

configurations may not allow users to download and install software, including plugin software. Additionally, plugin installation often requires that users visit other Web sites, which may not be accessible. And finally, many of the guidelines for universal usability are difficult, if not impossible, to implement using nonstandard formats.

Generally, the Web is most accessible when sites are built to standards. However, some sites require functionality that cannot be accomplished using standard Web coding. In these cases, apply the universal usability guidelines to the greatest extent possible, and provide alternate access for users who cannot access the nonstandard content.

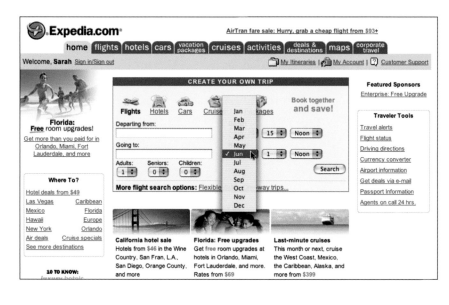

13.1 BASIC PRINCIPLES

13.1.1 Use add-ons for interactivity only when necessary

At times it may be useful for a Web page to update in response to user actions. For example, for a travel application, it would be useful if, after choosing a time frame for travel, the listing of available flights would update to show only flights available on those dates. This type of page-level interactivity is not native to the Web and can only be accomplished using add-ons such as Java, JavaScript, or Flash (**Figure 13.1**). Most current browsers support JavaScript natively, whereas other add-on technologies generally call for a plugin. Requiring a plugin for site access is risky, since many users will not have the plugin and may not be able, or will choose not, to install it.

In addition, many of the accessibility features that are built into HTML are not available in other formats. For example, structural markup is not part of the Flash format. Users cannot customize Flash content. However, designers can take measures to make nonstandard content accessible. Current versions of Flash allow designers to add accessibility features, such as alternate text for images and captions for audio. But ultimately, HTML is a more flexible and accessible format, and reliance on other formats means that more users will be unable to access and use site content.

Before moving away from standard HTML constructs, consider carefully: Is the desired functionality necessary, or could the same effect be accomplished using standard HTML? Page-level interactivity may be a more elegant way to address a task such as booking a flight, but the task could certainly be accomplished using standard coding (**Figure 13.2,** *previous page*).

For universal usability, we need to understand and work with the strengths and limitations of the medium before turning to other, less-accessible formats.

In a nutshell. Add-on technologies—such as JavaScript and Flash—are not as flexible or as accessible as HTML. Explore standard methods fully before resorting to a nonstandard format.

13.1.2 Allow users to control the user interface

Some interactive formats allow designers to take control of the user interface to a much greater extent than with HTML alone. Designers can modify the environment by opening new windows, resizing and repositioning windows, hiding browser toolbars, and moving the cursor focus (**Figure 13.3**). These functions are ordinarily part of the user's domain and so are defined by the user. When a page performs these functions on behalf of the user, usability suffers. Users may be disoriented by this new and inconsistent browser behavior, and the modifications may not fit users' needs.

For instance, designers can use JavaScript to open a new window, set its size and position, and determine which browser elements display—menus, toolbars, status bar, and so on. The new window can be defined as fixed or resizable. The user cannot override these settings. For example, if a designer uses JavaScript to open a page in a small, fixed-

FIGURE 13.3

Meetup provides help information (1) in small, auxiliary windows without navigation, status, or other standard browser toolbars (2).

size window, users who need large type will be forced to scroll and to read a narrow text column.

Another common technique is to move cursor focus from the top of the page, as is customary, to the search text input field. This action is based on the assumption that users want to search and that they will appreciate having the cursor in position to enter a query. Users who expect to access Web content starting at the top of the page—particularly people who use the keyboard to navigate, and those who use screen reader software—will be disoriented if the cursor is anywhere but at the top of the page.

Designers implement these functions for the sake of usability—to make Web use easier and more efficient. However, we need to recognize and respect the boundary surrounding the user's domain. The Web allows users to make decisions about their environment based on their needs and preferences. We can make Web use easier and more efficient *for more users* if we stick with conventional Web behaviors and allow users to control their own environment.

In a nutshell. Users become disoriented when the interface behaves in ways that are inconsistent with expectations. Do not assume control of elements of the interface that belong in the domain of the user, such as window size and cursor position.

13.1.3 Make interactivity keyboard-accessible

Interactivity is the inclusion of controls and elements that are actionable—those that trigger events when activated. Standard Web interactivity includes links and forms submission. Additional interactivity can be accomplished using add-ons such as JavaScript, QuickTime, and Flash. One of the key attributes of accessible interactivity is the mode in which events are triggered. Many times, interactive elements are designed to respond to mouse clicks: The user points the mouse and clicks to activate a control and trigger its associated event.

For universal Web access, all interactive elements must be designed to function using keyboard commands. Point-and-click interactivity is not possible for nonvisual users; such interactivity assumes a rendered page, and nonvisual users work with code. Other users cannot operate a pointing device and so rely on keyboard commands to work with the Web. An interactive element, such as a link or button, that cannot be activated using the keyboard is nonfunctional to such users.

As well as basic functionality, elements must function properly, behaving in a manner that is consistent with user expectations when operated from the keyboard. Keyboard navigation is a two-step process: a control is selected, and then activated. For example, using the tab key selects actionable elements, such as links and buttons. Pressing the enter key activates the selected link or button. This functionality must be standard with any interactive element, even when designed using a nonstandard format. Interactivity that is triggered using other actions will present problems for keyboard users.

A common example of an interactive control that does not follow standard practices is the select menu used to present quick links to site content. Often, these menus use the "select" action to activate: a page request is triggered when the user selects an item from the menu

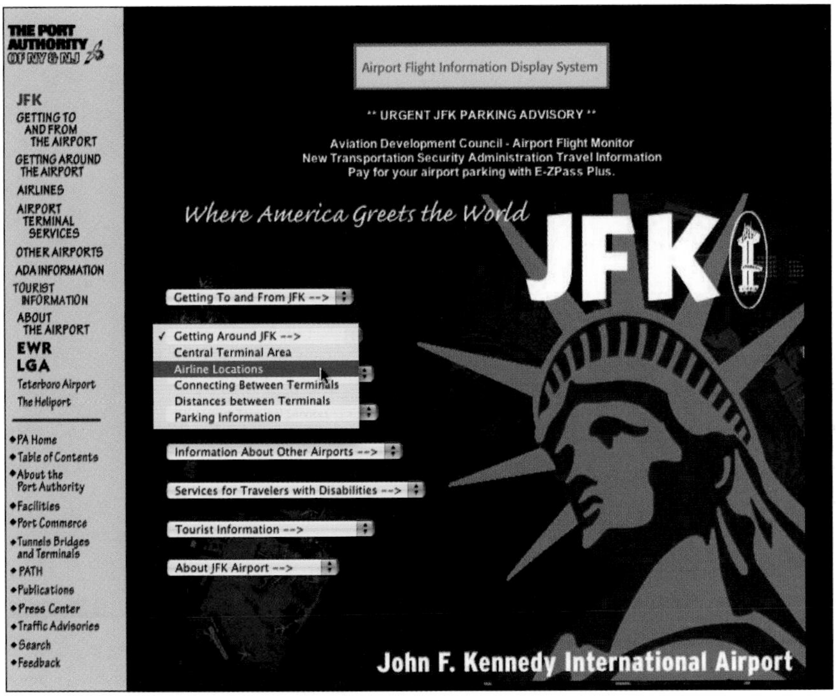

FIGURE 13.4
The John F. Kennedy International Airport home page uses dropdown menus to provide quick access to popular pages. The menus are activated by the "select" action—when a menu item is selected, the corresponding page is loaded. This type of point-and-click interaction is not usable from the keyboard.

(**Figure 13.4**). This approach assumes that the user will use a mouse to point to the desired menu item and then release the mouse, thereby selecting the item and triggering the event. Because keyboard users need to select and then activate, they never get past the first menu item. The menu is triggered by the select action, so once the first item is selected using the keyboard, its action is triggered and the corresponding page loads.

In a nutshell. Some users activate elements using the keyboard and will be unable to use an interface that requires point-and-click interaction. Make sure all interactive elements are usable from the keyboard and behave in a manner that is consistent with user expectations.

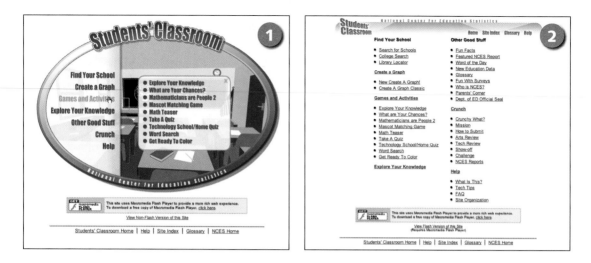

FIGURE 13.5
Sites that use Flash
exclusively for content
and navigation (1)
must provide an
HTML alternative (2).
Otherwise, users who
cannot access Flash will
be unable to use the site.

13.2 MARKUP

13.2.1 Provide an accessible alternate when using a nonstandard format

Not everything that appears on a Web page is essential to the user experience. For example, users do not necessarily need access to JavaScript rollovers to access the content of a Web site. The fact that an image highlights when rolled over by the mouse is not a functional necessity. Such rollover effects are generally used to provide visual interest, or to draw attention to functional elements such as links—not for essential site content. On the other hand, when site navigation is provided using Flash, users who do not have Flash installed, or who have difficultly accessing Flash-based content, will be unable to access the Web site (**Figure 13.5**).

Whenever providing essential functionality in a format that may be inaccessible to some users, provide the equivalent information as accessible HTML text (**Figure 13.6**). For example, when using Flash for navigation, provide alternate HTML text links for users who cannot access Flash. When using JavaScript for essential content, use the NOSCRIPT tag to provide equivalent content for users who cannot access JavaScript.

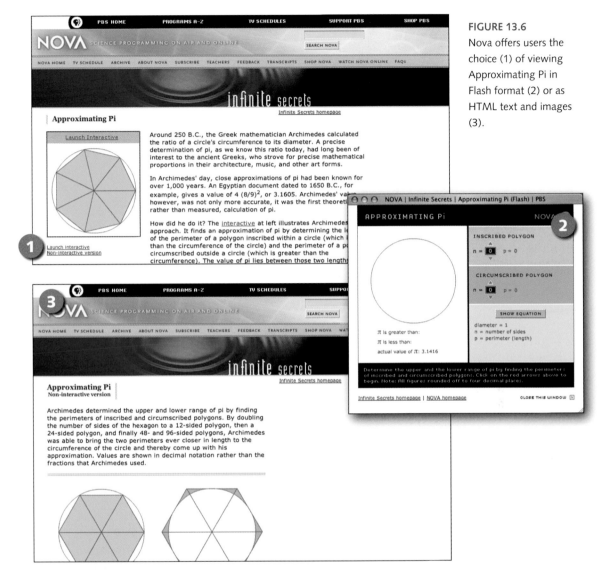

FIGURE 13.6
Nova offers users the choice (1) of viewing Approximating Pi in Flash format (2) or as HTML text and images (3).

In a nutshell. Some users cannot access interactivity designed using JavaScript or Flash. When providing content in a nonstandard format, provide the equivalent content as accessible HTML.

CHAPTER 14

Editorial Style

UNIVERSAL USABILITY DEMANDS an operable interface and accessible content. But for a Web site to be truly useful to all, it requires accessible language. Information must be presented in a manner that is usable and understandable.

Online readers approach Web text with specific methods and objectives. Some users skim a page to form an overview of the available information and options; others skim a page in search of specific information. Some read the information presented on the page, while others print Web pages and read them offline.

Web documents can be structured to support skimming in a number of ways. First, skimming works best when information is broken into segments. A single topic can be broken across several pages, and each page further broken into subsections. Editorial landmarks, such as headings and lists, can be used to emphasize important words and phrases. Skimming is further enhanced when the most visible elements—headings, links, lists—begin with key words and concepts.

The Web comes with a global audience that is impossible to accurately define. Web sites often have an *intended* audience, but the actual audience is almost certainly much broader. As a result, the best approach to writing for the Web is to write clearly and concretely, avoiding needless complexity and chatter. To address the diversity of a global audience, clarify concepts and terminology that may not be apparent to all users. Adopt a writing style and vocabulary and apply it consistently.

From a markup perspective, HTML provides a few simple tools to clarify text usage. Use the ABBR and ACRONYM tags to describe abbreviations, acronyms, and initialisms, and the LANG attribute to identify words, phrases, or paragraphs that are other languages.

FIGURE 14.1

IBM's Web Ease-of-Use Guidelines are written for online readers. The information is broken into segments marked by descriptive headings. Bulleted lists are used to emphasize important concepts and to facilitate scanning.

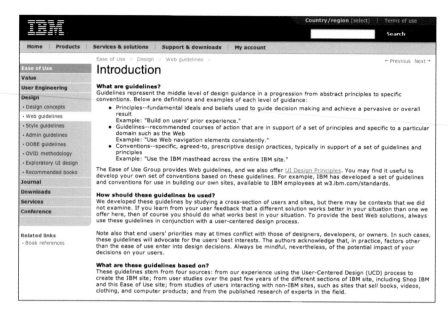

14.1 BASIC PRINCIPLES

14.1.1 Break up text into segments

Online readers tend to skim pages rather than read word by word. Skimming is easier when information is broken up into segments, and when headings are used to announce the subject of each segment. Within segments, lists and emphasis can help readers extract the most salient information (**Figure 14.1**).

Additionally, information can be broken into segments and presented over several Web pages. This approach provides direct access to subcategories of information. For example, software installation instructions might be broken across two pages entitled "Installation" and "Getting Started." Users who only want installation information can access that information directly, and vice versa.

This practice, commonly referred to as *chunking*, provides Web users with more direct access to the information they are seeking, and has the added benefit of producing shorter Web documents. However, users

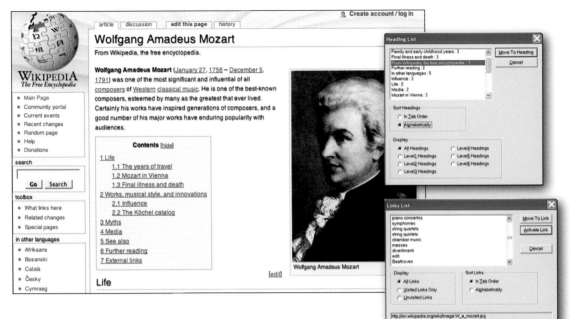

who prefer to read information offline might want to have all the information related to a topic on a single page for easier printing and downloading. Accommodate these users by including a single-page printing version.

In a nutshell. Web readers skim text to form an overview or to locate specific information. Break content into easy-to-skim segments, and use headings to identify the subject of each segment.

14.1.2 Start sentences, headings, and links with keywords

Web users generally skim new pages to get an overview of the available content and functionality. Skimming is more efficient when sentences begin with key words and phrases, particularly with regard to editorial landmarks, such as headings and links. In particular, screen reader software offers a page overview via a list option that displays a list of links or headings. The lists are displayed in alphabetical order, which makes the application of initial keywords particularly useful (**Figure 14.2**).

FIGURE 14.2
Wikipedia uses structural markup to identify headings, and uses keywords at the beginning of links and headings. This approach enhances the usability of software features, such as the Links List and Heading List features in JAWS, a screen reader program.

Initial keywords also come in handy when users are seeking a specific content item. For example, upon locating a keyword using the browser's find or "find-as-you-type" function, users will be positioned to continue reading if their search term is at the beginning of a heading or link.

In a nutshell. Skimming is more efficient when editorial landmarks begin with keywords. Put important words or phrases at the beginning of sentences, headings, and links.

14.1.3 Adopt a writing style that is clear and to the point

In *The Elements of Style,* William Strunk and E. B. White encourage writers to "use definite, specific, concrete language" and make "every word tell." There are few areas where this approach is more necessary than on the Web. As we have already established, most Web readers skim a page to form an overview of the content or to locate the specific word or phrase that corresponds to the information they are seeking. Nothing impedes this process more than vague, verbose language and meaningless prose. In general, Web users appreciate a writing style that uses the fewest words necessary to give a clear picture of the content and functions of a page.

The areas where clarity is most crucial are labeling and instructions—the elements that guide users through the functions of a page. Navigation is not a place for unclear language—link labels must be self-explanatory to guide users to their destination. Clarity in form labels is important, too. Ambiguous form labels lead to incorrect data. In general, all instructions should use clear and concise language.

Clear writing requires a discipline that few writers possess. Expressing a concept in a sentence or two is far more difficult than in a paragraph or page. However, clear writing is beneficial to usability and worth the extra effort.

In a nutshell. Web readers are goal-oriented and get bogged down by lengthy and unnecessary explanations and instructions. Be concise and factual; avoid meaningless prose.

14.1.4 Use appropriate language and terminology

Practically speaking, the Web audience is global and anonymous, making it impossible to truly "know" and target an audience with an appropriate writing style. Most sites cater to a specific audience: College and university sites cater to prospective and current students, e-commerce sites cater to consumers, reference sites cater to users with a specific knowledge level. For example, a programming reference site might be written specifically for intermediate to advanced programmers. However, that does not preclude beginners from accessing and learning from the materials on the site. Indeed, determining the interests, literacy, language, and knowledge level of the audience for any Web site can only be done in the most general terms. The best approach to targeting a diverse audience is to write with clarity and precision and without unnecessary complexity.

To determine an appropriate writing style, we must use terminology in a way that is meaningful to users. Whenever possible, establish the vocabulary by initially defining concepts and terms. Users who are familiar with the topic can skip over the foundational information and go directly to the more advanced materials, while users who are new to the topic can establish a foundation before advancing. Once terms are defined and put into service, apply them consistently throughout the site. Do not introduce new terminology to describe established concepts.

In some instances, one writing approach cannot be used for all audiences. For example, with health information, one style and vocabulary cannot meet the needs of both patients and practitioners who are seeking information about a particular disease or condition. When one size cannot fit all, include multiple versions targeted at different audience groups (**Figure 14.3,** *next page*).

In a nutshell. Users benefit from a writing style that is geared for their knowledge level. Adopt an appropriate writing style and vocabulary, and apply it consistently.

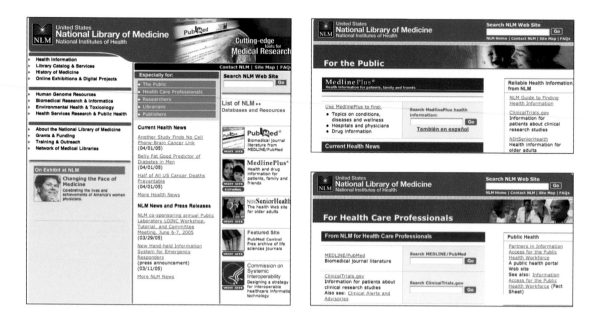

FIGURE 14.3

The National Library of Medicine offers medical information targeted at its different audience segments—the public, health care professionals, researchers, librarians, and publishers.

14.1.5 Keep content current and links functional

Nothing shakes the confidence of a Web user more than broken links and outdated content. Many Web pages announce events that occurred months prior, or reference out-of-date software, or publicize old news. Users encountering such pages quickly discern that the Web site has been neglected and is therefore unreliable.

Many Web designers do not appreciate that creating a Web site is a long-term commitment. Web sites need constant care and feeding if they are to thrive and be of value to users. Some sites are more static than others—for example, a reference or training site—whereas dynamic sites—like entertainment and news sites, and blogs—require fairly constant attention and upkeep. Even static sites need to be monitored for broken links.

Regular upkeep must be part of the design process to keep sites from falling into neglect. Keep content fresh and current, and monitor links to other sites.

In a nutshell. Out-of-date content and broken links put into question the overall reliability of a site. Revisit content on a regular basis to validate and repair links and to update or remove content.

14.2 MARKUP

14.2.1 Mark up language changes within a document

Web documents can have different languages within the same document, or different versions of the document in different languages. HTML markup allows designers to identify the primary language of the document, and to identify words or sections that are in other languages.

For example, if the primary language of a Web page is English, a French word or phrase can be identified as such using the LANG attribute: for example, `<span lang="fr">C'est la vie</span>`. The LANG attribute applies to different elements, such as links, paragraphs, headings, citations, and tables. When language changes are identified in the code of the page, software can use the information. For example, screen reader software can read the phrase with the appropriate pronunciation.

In order to mark language changes *within* a document, the primary document language must be identified by applying the LANG attribute to the HTML tag: for example, `<html lang="es">` for documents in Spanish.

In a nutshell. Software can read documents more accurately when language changes are identified. Indicate the primary document language, and use markup to mark language changes.

14.2.2 Identify and describe abbreviations and acronyms

HTML provides markup to describe abbreviations and acronyms so users who do not recognize, for example, the acronym *GIF* for *Graphics Interchange Format* or the abbreviation *px* for *pixels* can decipher the meaning. The difference between abbreviations and acronyms is that abbreviations are usually a shortened or condensed version of a word

FIGURE 14.4

The ABBR and
ACRONYM tags provide
a means to spell out
abbreviations and
acronyms. In this
Evolt.org article, the
term *CSS* is marked up
with the title, *Cascading
Stylesheets*. The title
appears when the user
positions the cursor over
the term.

or phrase—such as *ltd.* for *limited*, *inc.* for *incorporated*, *vol.* for *volume*, *ed.* for *edition*—whereas acronyms are pronounceable words formed using the initial letters of the words in a phase—such as *UNICEF* for the *United Nations Children's Fund* and *WAI* for the *Web Accessibility Initiative*. Initialisms—such as *UN* (*United Nations*) and *UPS* (*United Parcel Service*)—are pronounced as individual letters, and are best marked up as abbreviations since they are not acronyms.

When the ABBR and ACRONYM tags are used to markup up abbreviations and acronyms, the full version is available to both visual and non-visual users via the TITLE attribute (**Figure 14.4**). Additionally, screen reader software can be instructed when to spell out initialisms using HTML markup and aural style settings:

```
<abbr title="United Parcel Service"
    class="initialism">UPS</abbr>
.initialism { speak: spell-out; }
```

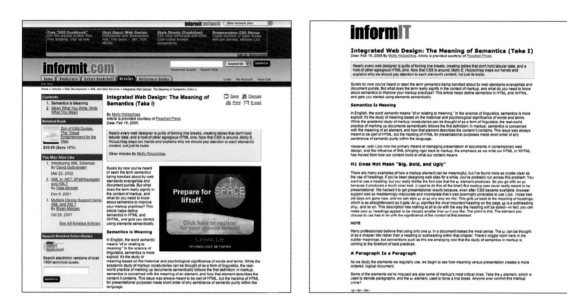

In a nutshell. Software can provide clarifying information for abbreviations and acronyms. For improved screen reader access, use style sheets to indicate whether these elements should be spoken or spelled out.

14.2.3 Provide a print option for lengthy documents

Some users prefer to read on paper rather than onscreen. They use the Web to locate information, print the resulting page, and read the printed document. When documents are broken up over several pages, these users must print several pages to reproduce the entire document.

When presenting documents that are likely to be printed, provide a single-page version for easier printing. Use styles or other methods to remove elements that are only useful in an online context, such as navigation links (**Figure 14.5**).

In a nutshell. Some people prefer to print longer documents for offline reading. Provide a single-page printing version for documents that are likely to be printed.

FIGURE 14.5
Some users prefer to print Web pages, particularly for extended reading. The InformIT site provides a single-page printing version of its articles without elements that are only relevant online, such as navigation links and search features.

Page Layout

W EB DESIGNERS HAVE MULTIPLE LAYERS to attend to. The visual layer is likely the one that gets the most attention and care, but Web design does not stop at the screen. To produce effective and functional designs that enable visual and nonvisual access, we must consider the visual characteristics of a page along with its underlying structure. The ultimate test of a Web page is how well it performs when read by software. This readability is influenced by the methods used to lay out pages.

Nonvisual access is contingent on the order in which elements appear in the code. Software reads Web pages from beginning to end. For pages to read well, elements must appear in logical sequence in the code. Related elements should be in close proximity and important content should appear at the beginning of the page. Pages that begin with layers of advertising, branding, and navigation links, or with content embedded within layout tables, do not read well.

When laying out a page visually, we use various design and typographic devices to identify and differentiate page elements, thereby revealing information structure. These cues must also be present for nonvisual access. When grouping related elements visually, make sure they are also grouped in the code. Use headings instead of visual text formatting to communicate information structure. Structural markup is the most effective way to communicate page structure to nonvisual users. Navigation links that are coded as a list are differentiated from other page elements by virtue of their enclosed markup.

Design simplicity and consistency are attributes that benefit all users. Too often Web sites are composed of pages that are overladen with navigation links and extraneous elements that get in the way of access. The elements used to establish the purpose and tenor of a Web site (logo, graphics), along with the elements used to operate it (navigation, search), must be balanced with the site content. Once a balanced design approach is established, the design should be applied consistently throughout so users learn the workings of a site once and can apply what they've learned to all pages.

Very often Web pages are designed to "optimal" dimensions based on the most common display resolution—800 × 600 or 1024 × 768. As more and more users access Web pages on a growing number of devices, this approach has become obsolete. For universal usability, page layouts must adapt to different viewing conditions. Building flexible pages using techniques that allow pages to adapt to different resolutions, zoom levels, colors, and so on, is the way to provide an optimal solution.

In creating a layout, style sheets offer the best solution for flexibility and device independence. As we have noted elsewhere, separating content and presentation allows users access to page content that is not tied to its presentation. This method holds true for page layout as well as content markup. Layouts that are designed using style sheets can be viewed on different devices using different style sheets.

15.1 BASIC PRINCIPLES

15.1.1 Design pages for linear access

Nonvisual access to Web pages is defined by the sequence in which elements appear in the underlying code. Software reads Web pages from top to bottom. For visual users, this linearity is of little consequence. Visual users can skim through a rendered page to locate the information they are seeking. Nonvisual users can also move around a Web page using software features such as link or heading lists, but generally the information at the beginning of the code will be the first to be "seen" by software. Keyboard access is also affected by the order of page elements, as the action of keys (such as the tab and arrow keys) begins at the top of the page—for example, the tab key cycles sequentially through links and form elements. Indexing software is also influenced by the order of

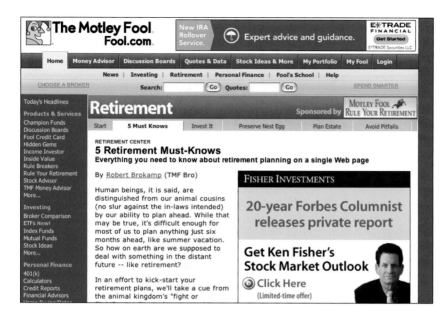

elements in code, giving more weight to content that appears toward the beginning of the page.

Web page design is only partially concerned with the way a page displays in the browser, though this aspect is perhaps the one that gets the most focus. The integrity and usability of the underlying structure is a large part of what defines the user experience. As designers, we need to attend to what displays on the screen, as well as the code that is responsible for the display, to design pages that are universally usable. And since the code defines the display, we cannot address these aspects of Web design independently.

Designing for linear access requires that we consider simultaneously the visual display and the code that is needed to create the display, with the goal of providing quick and easy access to content. Many of today's Web pages are not designed for linear access; the most common designs begin with advertising, branding, and extensive navigation (**Figure 15.1**). Users who are seeking content must skip over these elements to locate the main content of the page. For visual users, visual design may aid

FIGURE 15.2

A List Apart, Web Style Guide, and *Boxes and Arrows* put content close to the top of the page. Additionally, since the article headings are marked with heading tags, nonvisual users can use structure to locate the beginning of the articles.

A LIST APART

| up front | articles | about ala | live events | xml feeds |

ISSN: 1534-0295. 9 JANUARY 2004 – ISSUE NO. 167

Elastic Design

BY PATRICK GRIFFITHS

It can be difficult to move from a static, pixel-based design approach to an elastic, relative method. Properly implemented, however, elastic design can be a viable option that enhances usability and accessibility without mandating

Discuss
Talk about this article.

Bookmark
Permanent URI.

Not quite liquid, yet not fixed-width either, Elastic Design combines the strengths of both.

Web Style Guide
2ND EDITION

TYPOGRAPHY

Typography exists to honor content.
— Robert Bringhurst, *The Elements of Typographic Style*

TYPOGRAPHY is the balance and interplay of letterforms on the page, a verbal and visual equation that helps the reader understand the form and absorb the substance of the page content. Typography plays a dual role as both verbal and visual communication. As readers scan a page they are subconsciously aware of both functions: first they survey the overall graphic patterns of the page, then they parse the language, or read. Good typography establishes a visual hierarchy for

PROCESS

INTERFACE DESIGN

SITE DESIGN

PAGE DESIGN

TYPOGRAPHY
Characteristics of Web type
Structure & visual logic
• Cascading style sheets
Legibility

boxesandarrows

| CURRENT | PREVIOUSLY | CATEGORIES | AUTHORS | ABOUT |

Search

View Large Font Version | Print Preview | Discuss this Article   April 7, 2004

Read more articles in How to: Methods & Approaches

Card sorting: a definitive guide
by Donna Maurer and Todd Warfel

Introduction
Card sorting is a technique that many information architects (and related professionals.) use as an input to the structure of a site or product. With so many of us using the technique, why would we need to write an article on it?

While card sorting is described in a few texts and a number of sites, most descriptions are brief. There is not a definitive article that describes the technique and its variants and explains the issues to watch out for. Given the number of

"Card sorting is a great, reliable, inexpensive method for finding patterns in how users would expect to find content or functionality."

Recent Comments

Donna Maurer said:
" Casey, with your very brief description, I'd include the names of the software products (or th..."

October 11, 2004 04:20 AM

donna said:
" John, AIfIA has some spreadsheets in it's design tools collection that may be of use to you. ..."

June 5, 2004 07:20 PM

donna said:

this process if the main content area of the page is set off from other page elements. For nonvisual users, the process can be akin to finding a needle in a haystack. If the main content is not somehow identified in the code—for example, marked with a heading—nonvisual users must scan each element to determine where the page content begins.

One method for addressing this need is to provide nonvisual and keyboard users with a link that allows them to skip from the top of the page to the main content. However, the "skip navigation" or "skip to main content" link is a workaround. It allows us to maintain the design status quo without addressing the underlying problem: When we design pages that are top-heavy with nonessential content, the sequence of the code does not model user expectations. Given that code is accessed linearly, it makes sense to begin with important elements. For the majority of users, that most important element is content.

To optimize pages for linear access, begin with primary page content as opposed to advertising and navigation links; at minimum, put content as close as possible to the beginning of the page (**Figure 15.2**). Front-loading pages has many benefits, including better search indexing and improved access for screen reader and keyboard users.

In addition, pay close attention to the sequence of elements in the code. Related elements can be grouped visually on the rendered page but unconnected in code. This disconnect is common with layout tables, where related elements can be split into different table rows. We cannot rely solely on visual design to communicate relationships between elements. For universal usability, we must design using proximity and logical sequencing both visually and in the underlying code.

In a nutshell. Software reads the code of Web pages from top to bottom. Make sure the sequence of content is logical in the code. Put important content first, and group related content.

15.1.2 Communicate visual information to nonvisual users

Web design is concerned with both visual and nonvisual aspects of Web pages. One of the primary challenges is to make documents communicate

FIGURE 15.3

On the Wright Brothers online exhibition, site and section links are differentiated using proximity and contrast—serif text is used for site links (1, 2) and sans serif text for section links (3). Headings are differentiated from main text using contrast—the page heading is bold and serif (4), and the section headings are bold (5, 6).

both visually and nonvisually. Similar to building a structure, we need to attend to both the underlying structural components as well as the visual, surface elements, making sure information conveyed on the visual layer is also available in the document structure.

HTML has elements that may not display on screen but are nonetheless "visible" to software: alt-text for images; table elements, such as summary, cells, and rows; and title attributes for various page elements, such as images, frames, and links; among others. These built-in elements allow software to make sense of a page by identifying the purpose and content of visual elements.

Visual design helps communication. For instance, proximity reveals relationships between elements on a page. Related items are grouped together and set off from other elements by space or borders. Headings and labels are near the content they describe, such as section headings and table captions and legends. Typography and spacing provides additional

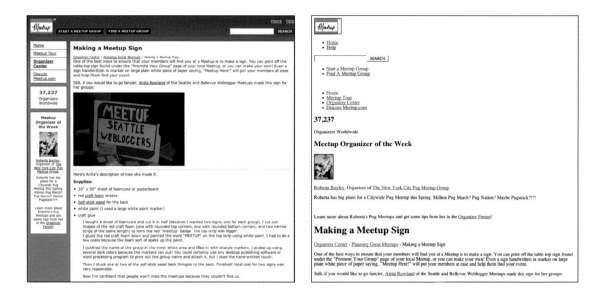

information, such as bolded headings and indented paragraphs. These design features help users understand page structure, which, in turn, leads to better understanding of the content (**Figure 15.3**).

For universal usability, Web documents must contain information about document structure in the code. When structure can be interpreted without the aid of visual design, documents can be read effectively by software. This requires that we consider our pages without visual cues and visual emphasis, without columns and proximity for grouping related content, without spacing and indents for communicating information hierarchy. We need to ensure that all information communicated via visual design is somehow represented in the underlying code.

Considering that Web pages are read in sequence, one way to communicate relatedness is to group related elements in the code. With complex designs using multiple layout tables, related content can easily get spread across different rows, creating a disjointed presentation when read by software. Pay attention to the sequencing of content in the code. Make sure the sequence is logical, and that related elements are grouped (**Figure 15.4**).

FIGURE 15.4

Proximity is a way of communicating the relatedness of page elements. The Meetup pages have different navigational elements grouped and located in different areas on the page. Since the links are similarly grouped within the page code, nonvisual users can also differentiate functional areas.

The best way to communicate information structure to nonvisual users is to use structural markup. Headings, paragraphs, lists, tables, and quotes can all be well described using structural markup.

Other elements are more difficult to communicate since no structural tags are available to describe them. For example, Web page navigation is easy to identify visually because it appears along the left or right margin as a list of links. However, HTML does not provide a structural tag for identifying navigation. Where HTML markup falls short, provide context through content—use page content to describe what is conveyed visually. For example, use titles to identify page links (such as, "On this page") and site links (such as, "In this site").

At times we need to communicate as little as possible about elements. For example, when layout tables are used, software will inform users that there is a table with x number of columns and rows, and will convey any additional information provided, such as summaries, headers, and captions. In this case, the less said, the better—in a layout table, a summary is unnecessary, as are structural tags such as TH and CAPTION. The same holds true for icons that are used to reinforce text. A right-facing arrow next to a "next page" link does not need to be described as "Right-facing arrow" in the image alt-text because its function is already described in the link. In this case, using alt="" in the image tag makes the image invisible to screen reader software (**Figure 15.5**).

In short, for visual and nonvisual Web page access, we must identify the essential elements in a design—the images, links, columns, and groupings that communicate the content and functional areas of a page—and make sure that these elements are represented both visually and in the code of the page.

In a nutshell. Some users cannot access information communicated via visual design. Make sure all relevant information that is communicated visually—through indents, spacing, proximity, and so on—is also conveyed in the code.

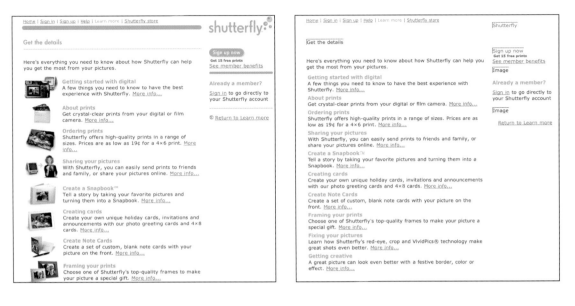

15.1.3 Apply a consistent design

Unlike other communication mediums, the Web has few, if any, design standards. Designers have no *Chicago Manual of Style* to advise them of best practices in Web design. Consequently, users have no consistent design conventions that they can rely upon to help them navigate the Web. Users must learn and relearn how to use the Web as the design and functional elements change from site to site and page to page.

All users benefit from the consistency that results from applied design conventions. Consider the common objects and devices that are part of everyday life. Consistent design of light switches, shovels, books, envelopes, potato peelers, elevators, doors, and so on, makes it possible for these items to be used without deliberation. Users approach these devices with an understanding of how they work, and can apply this understanding to all like devices. In short, design conventions allow users to focus on the task, not the medium.

As the Web matures, design conventions are evolving naturally. Pages generally begin with site identification via a logo and perhaps a tagline. The search function is often placed in the upper right corner.

FIGURE 15.5

This Shutterfly page uses images to visually reinforce text links. Providing the equivalent information via alternate text would be irrelevant and redundant for nonvisual users. In this case, blank alt-text (alt=" ") makes the image essentially invisible to nonvisual users.

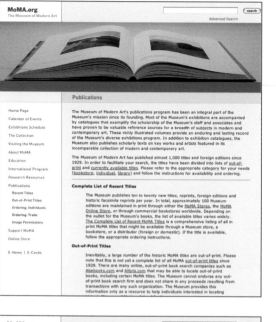

MoMA.org
The Museum of Modern Art

search
Advanced Search

Publications

Home Page
Calendar of Events
Exhibitions Schedule
The Collection
Visiting the Museum
About MoMA
Education
International Program
Research Resources
Publications
  Recent Titles
  Out-of-Print Titles
  Ordering: Individuals
  Ordering: Trade
  Image Permissions
Support MoMA
Online Store

E-News | E-Cards

The Museum of Modern Art's publications program has been an integral part of the Museum's mission since its founding. Most of the Museum's exhibitions are accompanied by catalogues that exemplify the scholarship of the Museum's staff and associates and have proven to be valuable reference sources for a breadth of subjects in modern and contemporary art. These richly illustrated volumes provide an enduring and lasting record of the Museum's diverse exhibitions program. In addition to exhibition catalogues, the Museum also publishes scholarly texts on key works and artists featured in its incomparable collection of modern and contemporary art.

The Museum of Modern Art has published almost 1,000 titles and foreign editions since 1929. In order to facilitate your search, the titles have been divided into lists of out-of-print and currently available titles. Please refer to the appropriate category for your needs (bookstore, individual, library) and follow the instructions for availability and ordering.

Complete List of Recent Titles

The Museum publishes ten to twenty new titles, reprints, foreign editions and historic facsimile reprints per year. In total, approximately 100 Museum editions are maintained in print through either the MoMA Stores, the MoMA Online Store, or through commercial bookstores worldwide. Depending on the outlet for the Museum's books, the list of available titles varies widely. The Complete List of Recent MoMA Titles is a comprehensive listing of all in print MoMA titles that might be available through a Museum store, a bookstore, or a distributor (foreign or domestic). If the title is available, follow the appropriate ordering instructions.

Out-of-Print Titles

Inevitably, a large number of the historic MoMA titles are out-of-print. Please note that this is not yet a complete list of all MoMA out-of-print titles since 1929. There are many online, out-of-print book search companies such as Abebooks.com and Alibris.com that may be able to locate out-of-print books, including certain MoMA titles. The Museum cannot endorse any out-of-print book search firm and does not share in any proceeds resulting from transactions with any such organization. The Museum provides this information only as a resource to help individuals interested in locating

---

MoMA.org
The Museum of Modern Art

search
Advanced Search

Publications | Complete List of Recent Titles

|A|B|C|D|E|F|G|H|I|J| |K-Z|

- A -

Allegories of Modernism
Bernice Rose
Paperback (1992)
Out of print

Alvar Aalto: Between Humanism and Materialism
Edited by Peter Reed; essays by Kenneth Frampton, Vilhelm Helander, Pekka Korvenmaa, Juhani Pallasmaa, Peter Reed, and Marc Treib
515 illustrations; 121 color illustrations
320 pages; hardcover (1998)
0-87070-107-X
Available
Trade Orders: North America-D.A.P.   Worldwide-Thames & Hudson
Individual Orders: MoMA

Alvar Aalto: Between Humanism and Materialism
Edited by Peter Reed; essays by Kenneth Frampton, Vilhelm Helander, Pekka Korvenmaa, Juhani Pallasmaa, Peter Reed, and Marc Treib
515 illustrations; 121 color illustrations
320 pages; paperback (1998)
0-87070-106-8
Available
Trade Orders: North America-D.A.P.   Worldwide-MoMA
Individual Orders: MoMA

An Afternoon in Astoria
Rudolph Buckhardt, introduction by Sarah Hermanson Meister
Hardcover (2002)
0-87070-436-2
Available
Trade Orders: North America-D.A.P.   Worldwide-Thames & Hudson
Individual Orders: MoMA

Laylah Ali
Illustrated throughout
36 pages, paperback (2002)
0-87070-362-x
Available
Trade Orders: North America-D.A.P.   Worldwide-MoMA
Individual Orders: MoMA

Manuel Alvarez Bravo

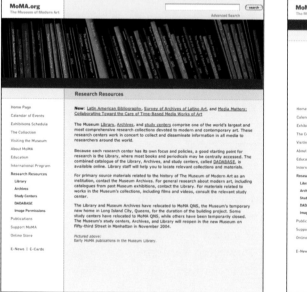

MoMA.org
The Museum of Modern Art

search
Advanced Search

Research Resources

Home Page
Calendar of Events
Exhibitions Schedule
The Collection
Visiting the Museum
About MoMA
Education
International Program
Research Resources
  Library
  Archives
  Study Centers
  DADABASE
  Image Permissions
Publications
Support MoMA
Online Store

E-News | E-Cards

New: Latin American Bibliography, Survey of Archives of Latino Art, and Media Matters: Collaborating Toward the Care of Time-Based Media Works of Art

The Museum Library, Archives, and study centers comprise one of the world's largest and most comprehensive research collections devoted to modern and contemporary art. These research centers work in concert to collect and disseminate information in all media to researchers around the world.

Because each research center has its own focus and policies, a good starting point for research is the Library, where most books and periodicals may be centrally accessed. The combined catalogue of the Library, Archives, and study centers, called DADABASE, is available online. Library staff will help you to locate relevant collections and materials.

For primary source materials related to the history of The Museum of Modern Art as an institution, contact the Museum Archives. For general research about modern art, including catalogues from past Museum exhibitions, contact the Library. For materials related to works in the Museum's collections, including films and videos, consult the relevant study center.

The Library and Museum Archives have relocated to MoMA QNS, the Museum's temporary new home in Long Island City, Queens, for the duration of the building project. Some study centers have relocated to MoMA QNS, while others have been temporarily closed. The Museum's study centers, Archives, and Library will reopen in the new Museum on Fifty-third Street in Manhattan in November 2004.

Pictured above:
Early MoMA publications in the Museum Library.

MoMA.org
The Museum of Modern Art

search
Advanced Search

Research Resources | Image Permissions

Home Page
Calendar of Events
Exhibitions Schedule
The Collection
Visiting the Museum
About MoMA
Education
International Program
Research Resources
  Library
  Archives
  Study Centers
  DADABASE
  Image Permissions
Publications
Support MoMA
Online Store

E-News | E-Cards

The Permissions Office of the Department of Imaging Services was founded in 1959. For 43 years, this office was responsible for the dissemination and licensing of images of the works of art in the Museum's collections, installation views of its exhibitions, and other archival material, for both study and publication. The Department of Imaging Services (originally "Rights and Reproductions") has set standards for the museum field in both licensing art for reproduction, and in imaging technology from black-and-white negatives and color transparencies and separations to its current, entirely digital workflow.

In order to more effectively service its clientele and market its images, The Museum of Modern Art has entrusted the licensing of images of works of art in its collections to Scala Archives of Florence, Italy. A world leader in the handling and marketing of color images related to art and culture, the Scala Picture Library contains some 80,000 works of art from renowned institutions around the world. Scala has offices in Florence, London, New York, and Tokyo. Scala and its New York representative, Art Resource, will provide high-resolution digital image files provided to them directly by the Museum's Imaging Studios.

All requests to reproduce works of art from MoMA's collection within North America (Canada, U.S., Mexico) should be addressed directly to Art Resource, Scala's New York representative, at 536 Broadway, New York, New York 10012. Telephone (212) 505-8700; fax (212) 505-2053, requests@artres.com, www.artres.com. Requests from all other geographical locations should be addressed directly to Scala Group S.p.A., 62, via Chiantigiana, 50011 Antella/Firenze, Italy. Telephone 39 055 6233 200; fax: 39 055 641124, archivio@scalagroup.com, www.scalarchives.it.

Requests for permission to reprint text from MoMA publications should be addressed to text_permissions@moma.org

---

Site navigation is often displayed across the top, and section navigation along the left or right column (**Figure 15.6**).

Usability is improved for all users when we apply conventions derived from communication and interface design. Constructing a model is far more difficult with a Web page than with a light switch or door. Upon arriving at a new Web site, users need to determine where they are, what they can expect to accomplish, what controls are available, where the content is located, and what other sections and pages are available. When we use standard conventions, users can use what they know as a point of reference and become oriented more quickly and effectively. If we apply conventions consistently, users need only orient themselves once—their model of a site can be applied to all pages.

The consistent application of design conventions is of particular benefit to nonvisual users. Nonvisual access to Web pages is in large part a linear process, which makes the type of overview required for mental modeling difficult to accomplish. The more these users can apply what they know about Web pages in general, the less they need to learn in order to use a specific Web page. Nonvisual users benefit when functional areas—content, navigation, search—are in consistent and therefore predictable locations.

In a nutshell. Users must learn how to use the Web at each site, and often within a single site, as the design and functional elements change from page to page. Adopt design conventions and a consistent navigation scheme for improved usability.

15.1.4 Balance content and navigation

Because the Web is both communication medium and software application, Web designers are challenged with the task of providing both meaningful content and a functional interface—all in the small window of a Web page. With well-designed pages, design decisions are made in support of achieving an appropriate balance between content and navigation, based on the nature of the site and the needs of its users.

FIGURE 15.6
(Facing page)
The MoMA site applies a consistent design to all its Web pages—navigation links in the left column, the search field in the upper right corner, and the section heading at the top of the page. Design consistency allows users to quickly form a model of the workings of a site and successfully apply it throughout the site.

Current Web pages tend to emphasize interface over content. Page designs often contain four or more navigation systems: *global navigation* for quick access to the main sections of the site, *local navigation* for access to the pages or subsections within the current section, *page navigation* for access to the sections on the current page, and *breadcrumb navigation* to show where the current page lies in the overall structure of the site, just to name a few. The purpose of navigation systems is to reveal possible destinations and, at the same time, to allow users to easily traverse from section to section, and page to page.

The primary rationale for navigation systems is that they minimize the number of clicks needed for users to reach their destination. For example, a clothing site might offer navigation links to all clothing categories, allowing users to go from "Shorts" to "Sweaters" in one click without having to backtrack to the home page (**Figure 15.7**).

Pages with extensive navigation options suffer the same disease as many of today's devices—feature creep. Feature creep occurs when features are added to a design because technically they can be added, and because they might be useful. The net result is a complex, multilayered device that is difficult to use. Link creep works the same way. When multiple links are added to a page *just in case* a user might want to go from *a* to *b*, the many users who don't find those links relevant and useful are forced to work through a cluttered page to find the relevant link or information.

Navigation is certainly useful, but must be designed intelligently. Chances are a user shopping for shorts is not also shopping for sweaters, but instead sandals or swimsuits. Shoppers need ready access to account information and a shopping cart, but perhaps not information about the company or store locations. Navigation systems that are context-sensitive—that provide appropriate links based on content and available tasks—are more effective than extensive link lists covering every possible eventuality. Some backtracking is reasonable, particularly given that many users use the back button as their primary navigation device. Users who *do* want to go from "Shorts" to "Sweaters" can backtrack to "Men's clothing" and go from there.

Minimizing navigation helps all users. Visual users aren't overwhelmed or disoriented by unnecessary page elements. Nonvisual users do not have to work through elements that are irrelevant to the content of the page. And with contextual navigation, users have appropriate options on hand when they need them (**Figure 15.8,** *next page*).

In a nutshell. Many links make for busy, overwhelming pages. Rather than overload pages with navigation options, focus on presenting content and context-sensitive navigation.

FIGURE 15.8
MayoClinic.com
makes good use of
contextual linking on
its articles pages. In this
article, each section is
followed by links to
other MayoClinic.com
articles that relate to the
information covered in
the section.

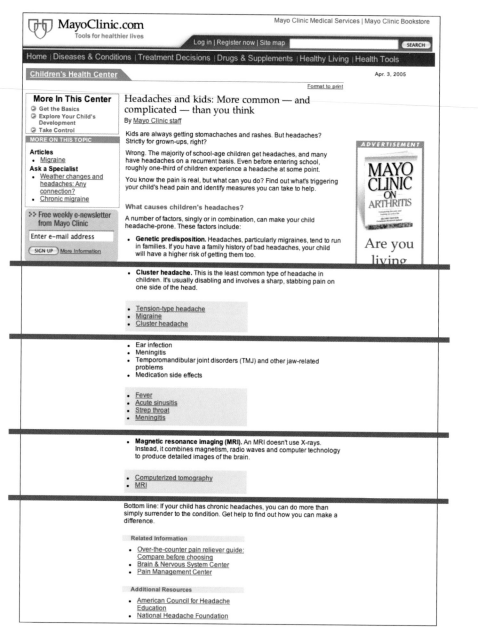

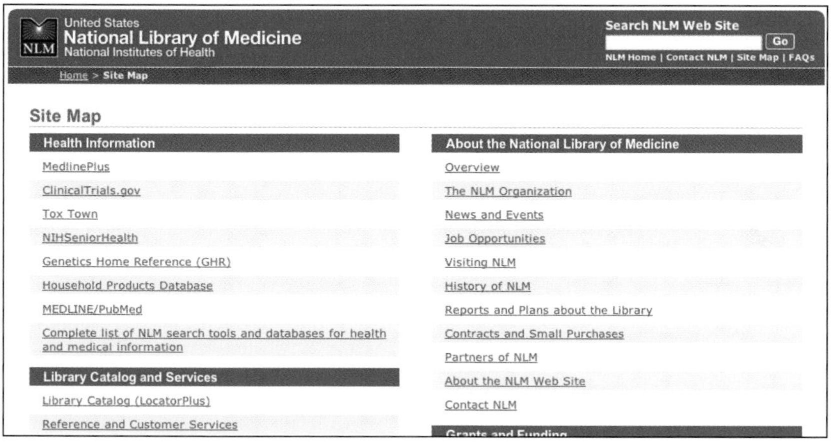

FIGURE 15.9
The CDC A-Z Index is useful for users who want information about a specific topic. The National Library of Medicine Site Map provides an overview of the site contents, as well as direct access to specific topics.

15.1.5 Provide navigation tools

One of the greatest challenges facing Web users is finding the page that contains the information or functionality they are seeking. Navigation systems can point the way, but even a well-structured, user-centered navigation design is bound to fail at times. Questions will arise about a site's information architecture and labeling system: for example, is location information under "About us" or "Contact us"? Is pricing information under "Products" or "Buy online"? Some ambiguity is unavoidable—designing an information architecture and labeling system that maps perfectly to all user expectations is impossible. When users cannot locate what they are seeking using page-based navigation systems, specialized navigation tools can be of use.

A number of navigation tools will work for different types of users and for different types of tasks. A reliable search function is useful for goal-oriented users who know what they are looking for. These same users also benefit from a site index that lists all site content alphabetically. A hierarchical outline of site categories, sometimes called a "site map," provides a site overview to help users determine where the page they are seeking lies within the overall site architecture (**Figure 15.9**, *previous page*). Another useful navigation tool is a quick links menu with links to commonly sought-after pages. This allows users to bypass navigation altogether and go directly to the page they are seeking.

In a nutshell. Users often have difficulty finding what they are seeking. Provide tools to help users locate content, such as search, site index, site map, and quick links.

15.2 MARKUP

15.2.1 Design flexible page layouts

Web pages are inherently accommodating. Left to their own devices, page layouts adapt to fit the browser window. The flexibility of Web layouts worked relatively well in the early days of the Web, when pages were mostly single-column text documents that could hold their design at different widths. Once graphics made their way onto Web pages, size began to matter. A 600-pixel-wide image needs 600 pixels of width to render, whereas a line of text can reflow to adapt the window width. Layout tables were then "invented," making true page layout possible, and fixed designs of a certain optimal width became the norm. A fixed-width design approach works well for complex, multicolumn layouts because it offers control over column widths and line wrapping. A complex layout is difficult to design with moving elements—for example, a

button bar that wraps at a narrow window width. Fixed design forces a minimum width to preserve the integrity of the design.

A flexible, or "liquid," approach to page layout attempts to accommodate the diversity of display environments. Rather than serving only the "most common" display dimensions and the "typical" user, a flexible layout adapts to different viewing conditions and different user requirements. Flexible layouts are far more difficult to design than fixed layouts because elements need to be able to change shape and position without jeopardizing the integrity of the overall page design.

Design is often about compromise. In the case of fixed layout, the main compromise is that users cannot "unfix" a fixed layout—users cannot somehow extract page content and place it into a flexible wrapper that allows them to scale the text or to change the window width to better accommodate their needs or viewing conditions. With a fixed-width, multicolumn layout, users who enlarge text may have to contend with columns containing three or four words per line. Users viewing a fixed-width layout on a small display may have to use the horizontal scroll to access a full line of text (**Figure 15.10**). Both of these circumstances present significant usability challenges that cannot be resolved by the user.

FIGURE 15.10
CNET uses a fixed-width design intended for 1024-pixel-wide displays. Users with smaller monitors will be forced to scroll horizontally to see the full extent on the page.

In the case of flexible design, the main compromise is that users are sometimes presented with long lines of text that are difficult to read. Typographic conventions suggest that a column width that produces approximately 66 characters per line is a comfortable line length, or *measure*. Long lines affect readability—the greater the distance from right margin to left, the more difficult it is to locate the next line when reading. When text is displayed in a flexible layout, line length is determined by the width of the browser window. A large display with a maximized browser window will likely result in long lines (unless the user has enlarged text), in which case, the user must either deal with long lines or narrow the browser window to a more comfortable measure.

The fundamental difference between the compromises that accompany these two layout methods is user control. With fixed design, users who need a different page width have no recourse, whereas with flexible design, users set page width by adjusting the width of the browser window. Moreover, it is important to note that conventions such as line length are meaningful in a fixed medium such as book design, where type size and line length cannot be altered. However, these conventions do not hold up in the Web environment, where users control type size, typeface, and column width, and are using a growing multitude of devices to access the Web, each with different screen dimensions and resolutions. On the Web, design is a moving target. A 66-character line on one display, resolution, and text size may be a 20-character line on another. A designer can only "suggest" attributes such as type size and line length. Besides, enforcing conventions using fixed design methods prevents access for users who may not fit the "average" profile.

Flexible layouts are the best page design approach for universal usability. Flexible pages adapt to different viewing conditions and respond to user control. To create a flexible layout, use relative measurements, such as percentages, to define the attributes of page elements—for example, set the banner width to 100%, the navigation column width to 20%, the main content column to 80%, and the footer width to 100%.

Watch out for page elements that require a width window to display properly, such as a banner graphic or navigation tabs. Favor small images that do not require a wide page to display properly.

In a nutshell. Users who enlarge type or view pages on a small display need a flexible layout that will adapt to their viewing environment. Design flexible layouts using relative measurements.

15.2.2 Use style sheets for layout whenever possible

Flexibility is what sets the Web apart from other communication and information technologies as a medium for universal usability. Information contained in a fixed medium—such as a newspaper, book, television program, or street sign—cannot adapt to the requirements of the user. The designer of a book must make decisions about aspects of the book. Inevitably, the decisions will interfere with access. For example, some users will find the text size too small for reading. The designer of a Web page must also make design decisions, and the decisions may also affect access for some users. However, because the Web is a flexible medium, users can adapt designs to meet their access requirements—if the text is too small, the user can enlarge it. Transformations need not be limited to altering text size. When style sheets are used for layout, almost all aspects of a Web page design can be transformed.

Maximum flexibility comes from a total separation of content and presentation—when content is contained in a structured HTML document and presentation is handled via style sheets. Pages cannot be easily transformed when styles are not used to define page layout. Layout features, such as columns and positioning, must be defined along with content in the HTML document. In this case, content and presentation are bound together, and transformations are difficult, if not impossible, to achieve. On the other hand, layouts that are defined using structural markup and style sheets are highly adaptable. Since the layout information is separate from the content, pages can be easily transformed by applying different style settings. Users can access pages without any

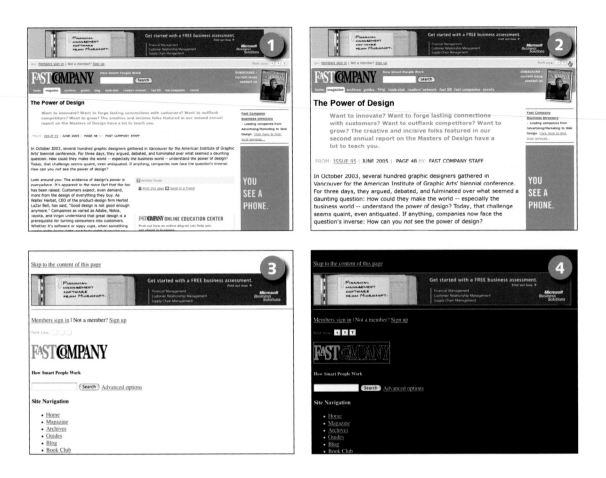

styling, or by using their own custom style sheet (**Figure 15.11**). Pages can have different layouts depending on the access device used—a PDA may use one layout and a computer display another. Sites can offer different views—print, large text, text only, and high contrast—simply by switching style sheets.

In a nutshell. Flexibility is best achieved when content and presentation are separate. Design pages using structural markup, and use style sheets to control page layout.

15.2.3 Provide direct access to page content

Linear access to Web pages can be cumbersome when Web pages are top-heavy with nonessential elements, such as branding and advertising. Nonvisual users and keyboard users cannot easily move the cursor to different functional areas of a Web page, but instead must work through page elements in sequence. Users who are after the main content of the page must work though the branding and navigational elements to locate the content, and must repeat this process as they move from page to page.

The best way to reduce the tedium of linear access is to put the important information close to the top of the page. Content that appears at or close to the beginning of the code is easier to locate and has the added benefit of increasing search quality. Search engine software uses location as a measure for determining the subject of a page—content that appears at the beginning of a page is considered to be the most relevant. Users who want direct access to navigation, not content, have options because links are easier to locate than content. Nonvisual and keyboard users can locate links more easily than content because links are actionable and can be accessed directly via the tab key or through software features such as the link list. "Content" is not an HTML structure; software therefore cannot provide a "jump to content" feature since it cannot locate anything tagged as "content" on the page.

HTML does provide heading tags. Specialized software, such as screen reader software, often provides heading navigation and a headings list. When the main content area of a page begins with an H1 heading describing the content of the page, users can move to the content area by navigating to the heading. Providing direct access to content via heading tags is a good and practical use of document structure. However, users of most standard browser software currently do not have access to this feature.

Sometimes visual design calls for page elements—such as navigation—to appear before page content. When styles are used for layout, the visual order of elements need not interfere with the sequence of elements in the code. Good linear access can be maintained because

FIGURE 15.11

(Facing page)

Fast Company uses style sheets for layout, making pages easy to adapt by applying different styles. Users can choose different font sizes (1, 2) using the built-in font-size switcher, or choose to view pages without styles (3) or with a custom style sheet (4).

styles determine the order of elements on the screen. For example, the sequence of elements in the code may be banner, content, navigation, and footer, but on screen the navigation may appear in the left column before the content area (**Figure 15.12**).

Some designs may not allow for quick access to content in the code—for instance, designs that require layout tables, or that require elements to appear in a certain order (for example, advertising first), or legacy designs that cannot be altered. Whenever content may be difficult to access from the code, provide a link to allow users to skip directly to the content area. The "Skip to main content" or "Skip navigation" link is a convention that has evolved as designs become more top-heavy, making it challenging for keyboard users to arrive at the main content area of a page. The skip link is placed at the beginning of the page and links to an anchor that is located at the main content area. When a user activates the link, the cursor focus moves from the link to the anchor. Page access resumes from the main content area location.

In order to be usable by both visual and nonvisual keyboard users, the skip link must display on the page. Skip links are often coded so they are not visible on screen—the link is sometimes attached to a transparent image, or made "invisible" through styling or by placing the link off screen. A nondisplaying skip link is accessible to screen reader software since it appears in the code. However, visual keyboard users may not realize the link is available and will have to cycle through all the elements at the beginning of the page to access the content. A visible skip link provides the means for both visual and nonvisual users to skip directly to the main content area.

In a nutshell. Pages that begin with nonessential content can prove cumbersome for some users. Place content close to the top of each page, marked by a heading. Alternatively, provide a visible "Skip to main content" link at the beginning of each page.

FIGURE 15.12

Style sheet positioning can be used to arrange elements on screen in a different order than they appear in the code. Blogger uses styles to position the main content of the page to the right of customer feedback. However, in the code of the page, the content appears before the feedback.

Acknowledgments

WHEN I ASKED MY FRIEND Karen Gocsik to be my development editor, I expected her to smooth the rough edges and keep me on track. However, Karen is a teacher above all else—and an excellent one. Somehow, in all the back-and-forth of editing and revising, she taught me to be a better writer. This book reflects her expertise and excellence, as well as the steadfast support she provided throughout.

Glenn Fleishman, my technical editor, has been my friend for many years. Glenn helped set this book in motion, and later gave it an exacting and expert technical review. I am grateful to Glenn for putting me through my paces and making this a better book. I continue to be impressed by the energy and knowledge he brings to all he does.

Much of what I know about interface design I learned from Ben Shneiderman. Ben helped establish the field of human-computer interaction and has advocated user-centered design throughout his career. In researching this book, I discovered that Ben's current research is focused on the universal user. His articles on universal usability and his most recent book, *Leonardo's Laptop: Human Needs and the New Computing Technologies,* have provided me with both information and inspiration. I am honored by his willingness to contribute to this book, and grateful for his encouragement along the way.

I am grateful to the members of the WebAIM (Web Accessibility in Mind) mailing list. Their willingness to answer questions, clarify concepts, and explore alternatives has taught me much of what I know about the practical application of universal usability. I also thank Andrew Kirkpatrick of the WGBH National Center for Accessible Media for his ready responses to my queries. Lou Rosenfeld encouraged me early on to write this book—I am grateful for the push. And, as always, I thank Pat Lynch for his tutelage, friendship, and support.

To the organizations and individuals whose work appears on the pages of this book, thank you for contributing to this effort. I am especially indebted to the many governmental organizations whose public domain work is shown here—thank you for providing so many excellent examples.

At Peachpit Press, I thank Nancy Davis, Marjorie Baer, Karyn Johnson, Rebecca Ross, Mimi Heft, Hilal Sala, Doug Adrianson, Beverly Bitagon, Kim Lombardi, and Mimi Vitetta for their excellence and hard work.

At Dartmouth, I thank Nancy Pompian for insight and inspiration. Every time I talk to Nancy she introduces me to something new, and it was Nancy who introduced me to the concept of universal design. I am grateful to my colleague Barbara Knauff for reading my drafts and keeping me consistent. I also thank my other friends and colleagues at Dartmouth—Malcolm Brown, Jeff Bohrer, Sheila Culbert, Karen Gocsik, Martha McDaniel, Elizabeth Polli, Mark O'Neil, and Susan Simon—for their encouragement and support.

I am grateful to all the Web designers, developers, and enthusiasts who are part of my world, both online and off—thank you for sharing your knowledge and enthusiasm.

I thank my large family for their patience and encouragement. Especially, I thank my two favorite guys: Malcolm, for keeping the home fires burning, and Nico, for bringing me such good luck.

ABOUT THE AUTHOR

Sarah Horton is a Web developer with Academic Computing at Dartmouth College, where she helps faculty incorporate technology into their teaching. Together with Patrick Lynch she authored the best-selling *Web Style Guide*, currently in its second edition. The online version of *Web Style Guide* has been available since 1994 and is often cited as *the* source for learning good Web design. *The New York Times* called *Web Style Guide* "an *Elements of Style* for Webmasters" (Jude Biersdorfer). Her second book, *Web Teaching Guide*, was the 2000 winner of the American Association of Publishers Award for the Best Book in Computer Science. Sarah has written articles about Web accessibility and usability in various publications, including *The New York Times, Boxes and Arrows, Digital Web Magazine, Syllabus,* and *IEEE Computer.* Sarah regularly speaks on the topic of creating usable and accessible Web sites.

ABOUT THE DEVELOPMENTAL EDITOR

Karen Gocsik is associate director of the Writing Program at Dartmouth College, where she also teaches composition. Karen works actively as a textbook editor, script doctor, screenwriter, and producer. Two of her films—*Because of Mama* and *From the 104th Floor*—premiered at the Sundance Film Festival before going on to screen and win acclaim at festivals around the world. She lives in Vermont with her daughters.

ABOUT THE TECHNICAL EDITOR

Glenn Fleishman is a freelance technology reporter who contributes regularly to *The New York Times, The Seattle Times, Mobile Pipeline,* and *Macworld* magazine. He is a contributing editor at TidBITS, and writes the editorial Weblogs Wi-Fi Networking News and Droxy.com on digital radio. Glenn founded one of the first Web development firms in 1994, worked for Amazon.com for six years before it went public, and has been designing and updating usable and accessible sites his entire Web career. He lives in Seattle with his wife and son.

ABOUT BEN SHNEIDERMAN

Ben Shneiderman is a professor in the Department of Computer Science, founding director (1983–2000) of the Human-Computer Interaction Laboratory, and member of the Institute for Advanced Computer Studies and the Institute for Systems Research, all at the University of Maryland at College Park. He was elected as a fellow of the Association for Computing Machinery (ACM) in 1997 and a fellow of the American Association for the Advancement of Science (AAAS) in 2001. He received the ACM SIGCHI Lifetime Achievement Award in 2001.

Ben is the author of *Designing the User Interface: Strategies for Effective Human-Computer Interaction* (4th ed., 2004, with C. Plaisant). With S. Card and J. Mackinlay, he coauthored *Readings in Information Visualization: Using Vision to Think* (1999). With B. Bederson he coauthored *The Craft of Information Visualization* (2003). His book *Leonardo's Laptop* appeared (MIT Press, 2002) won the IEEE book award for Distinguished Literary Contribution.

Appendix

Fundamentals

1.1 BASIC PRINCIPLES

1.1.1 Design simply
Simple designs are easier to use and maintain. Design simple sites, emphasizing important elements and using simple structures and clean, standards-based markup.

1.1.2 Build well
The Web has properties that enable universal access. Take full advantage of these inherent properties, such as fallbacks, flexibility, and user control, to construct universally usable Web sites.

1.1.3 Favor HTML over other formats
HTML is the best format for universal usability. Provide documents in nonstandard formats, such as PDF and Flash, only as an alternative to accessible HTML.

1.2 MARKUP

1.2.1 Design for keyboard access
Some users navigate the Web using the keyboard only. Make sure all functional elements, such as links and forms, can be controlled and activated from the keyboard.

1.2.2 Design for transformation

Web pages adapt to the user environment and user modifications. Design pages that adapt to different conditions, such as enlarged text or different window widths, while keeping their design integrity.

1.2.3 Allow users to control their environment

Web users have control over many aspects of their environment. Do not take control of aspects of the user interface, such as text size and link underlines, that belong in the domain of the user.

Document Structure

2.1 BASIC PRINCIPLES

2.1.1 Separate content and presentation

Content that is encoded without display requirements can be accessed by any software or device. Use HTML documents for content, and CSS for presentation.

2.1.2 Mark up document structure

Semantic markup produces content that can be read and *interpreted* by software. When encoding content, tag the meaning of document elements using structural HTML.

2.1.3 Use style sheets for presentation

Style sheets provide control and flexibility for designers and users. Use style sheets to control the presentation of Web pages.

2.1.4 Design pages that function without style sheets

Some users do not access styles. Design pages that are comprehensible and usable without style sheet formatting.

2.2 MARKUP

2.2.1 Write valid code
Valid code is essential to solid document structure. Identify document type and validate pages to ensure quality and compatibility.

2.2.2 Use linked style sheets
Linked style sheets promote design consistency and produce faster downloads. Include style information in a linked style sheet rather than on each Web page.

Text

3.1 BASIC PRINCIPLES

3.1.1 Use plain text for text
Text has many benefits over other content formats: it can be read by software, it adapts to different user environments, and text supports user customization. Whenever possible, favor text over other content formats.

3.1.2 Use CSS for styling text
Style sheets provide the greatest flexibility for styling and customizing text display. Use style sheets to define text's visual properties—font, size, color, and so on.

3.2 SIZE

3.2.1 Allow user settings to define base text size
Users should define their optimal text size setting. Allow the main text of a page to size according to the user-defined setting.

3.2.2 Size other text elements relative to the user-defined text size

Relative measurements—such as percentages and ems—size elements relative to their parent element. Use relative measurements for type variants—such as headings and links—so they size relative to the user-defined text setting.

3.2.3 Design pages that can accommodate different text sizes

Users must be able to resize text and still have a functional page. Design flexible pages so users can resize text without breaking the layout.

3.3 COLOR

3.3.1 Maintain contrast between text and background

Low-contrast color combinations interfere with readability. Use complementary colors and brightness values—such as black and white or purple and yellow—to produce the highest contrast between text and background.

3.3.2 Use style sheets for setting text color

Not all color combinations work for all users. Define colors using style sheets so people who need certain color combinations—such as white on black or yellow on black—can apply a custom style sheet.

3.3.3 Do not use text color alone to convey information

Color is not universally accessible and therefore cannot be relied upon as the sole means of conveying information. Pair other methods—such as typography or text—with color to convey emphasis or information.

3.4 MARKUP

3.4.1 Mark up text using structural tags

Structural markup adds meaning to documents. Use structural tags—H1–H6, P, EM, STRONG, and so on—to describe the meaning and function of text elements.

3.4.2 Use structural markup appropriately

Structural integrity requires that tags be used appropriately and consistently. When marking up text using structural markup, use the tag that accurately describes the element.

Images

4.1 BASIC PRINCIPLES

4.1.1 Use images purposefully

Images come at a cost to usability—they take time to download and are inaccessible to users who cannot see them. Use images with a purpose, such as providing information or enhancing the user interface.

4.1.2 Do not use graphic text

Graphic text is not machine-readable, flexible, or customizable, and therefore is inaccessible to some users. Avoid using graphic text; use plain text instead.

4.1.3 Avoid animated images

Animations are distracting and can even be debilitating. Avoid using animations. When using animations, allow users to control playback: play, pause, and stop.

4.2 TEXT ALTERNATES

4.2.1 Provide alt-text for all relevant images

Users who cannot access images can get the equivalent information via alt-text. For images that are part of the user interface, use alt-text to provide the functional equivalent, such as "Go to next page" or "Print this page." For content images, use alt-text to provide a brief image description.

4.2.2 Provide a full text description for content images

Content images may require more description than can be provided via alt-text. Provide a text description of the image information using a linked page or image caption.

4.2.3 Provide blank alt-text for irrelevant or redundant images

Not all images are relevant to nonvisual users. When images are not relevant outside of a visual context—such as spacer images or custom bullets—provide blank alt-text (alt="").

4.2.4 Maintain a catalog of image content

Alt-text and text descriptions are integral to providing image-based content. Maintain an image inventory that includes alt-text and text descriptions, particularly for large-scale or collaborative projects.

4.3 SIZE

4.3.1 Keep image dimensions as small as possible

Large images take longer to download and limit page flexibility. Keep image dimensions as small as possible, and save images using as much compression as possible without significantly degrading image quality.

4.3.2 Use thumbnails for large images

Large images are sometimes integral to the purpose of a site. Provide access to large images using thumbnails or text links so users can choose whether to load the image.

Data Tables

5.1 BASIC PRINCIPLES

5.1.1 Use table markup for data
Structural integrity requires that tags be used appropriately. Avoid using tables for layout; use tables to mark up tabular information.

5.1.2 Simplify data table layouts
Complex data tables can be challenging to navigate for both visual and nonvisual users. Present tabular information in its simplest form for easier scanning and screen reader access.

5.2 MARKUP

5.2.1 Identify data table row and column headings
Table headings are essential for establishing context for the data contained within the rows and columns of a table. Code tables so row and column headings are explicitly tied to the data they describe.

5.2.2 Use CAPTION and SUMMARY to describe data tables
Provide additional context by using `CAPTION` and `SUMMARY` tags to tie descriptive information about data tables to the tables they describe.

Layout Tables

6.1 BASIC PRINCIPLES

6.1.1 Use tables for layout only when necessary
Table markup is designed to describe tabular data and not for laying out pages. Use style sheets for page layout whenever possible; fall back on table layout only as a last resort.

6.1.2 Use simple layout tables

Layout tables can be disorienting for nonvisual users when related elements are spread across table rows and nested tables. Design simple layouts using simple layout tables.

6.2 MARKUP

6.2.1 Use only basic table tags

Screen reader software cannot distinguish between "real" tables and layout tables, making table markup difficult for nonvisual users to ignore. Make layout tables as unobtrusive as possible, using only basic table tags, such as TR and TD.

6.2.2 Design layout tables for linear access

Software reads page elements in the sequence that they appear in the code. Make certain the logical information flow of the rendered page—banner, navigation, content, and footer—is reflected in the code.

6.2.3 Use flexible cell widths

Flexible layouts adapt to different viewing conditions. Use flexible measurements—such as percentages—to specify the width of table cells so pages will adapt to accommodate different displays and text sizes.

Frames

7.1 BASIC PRINCIPLES

7.1.1 Avoid using frames

Standard behaviors—such as printing, bookmarking, and returning to a previous page—behave differently with frames-based pages than with standard Web pages and therefore cause usability problems for all users. Avoid using frames.

7.2 MARKUP

7.2.1 Use frame titles to identify the function of each frame

Nonvisual users may have difficultly navigating a frames-based page without some idea of the contents and function of each frame. Use frame titles—such as "Banner," "Navigation," and "Content"—to label each frame so nonvisual users can differentiate and navigate between frames.

7.2.2 Provide an alternative to frames

Some users opt not to use frames or to use a browser that does not support frames. Use the NOFRAMES tag to provide alternate access to framed content: for example, provide access to site navigation via the NOFRAMES tag.

Lists

8.1 BASIC PRINCIPLES

8.1.1 Use list markup for lists

Lists are a common element in Web page designs—most notably, navigation is a list of links. Use list mark-up for lists and use style sheets to control their visual properties.

8.1.2 Avoid compound lists

Compound lists can be disorienting and difficult to decipher, particularly for nonvisual users. Break compound lists into sections marked by headings, or use numbering to indicate the relationships between list items.

Forms

9.1 BASIC PRINCIPLES

9.1.1 Design simple and clear forms
Forms are often difficult to complete because of needless complexity and unclear instructions. Design for clarity and simplicity so users can complete forms successfully.

9.1.2 Provide an alternate to forms
Web forms may not satisfy the needs of all users. At minimum, provide an email address as an alternate method to communicate and interact with users who cannot or choose not to use forms.

9.2 MARKUP

9.2.1 Label form fields
Field labels tell users what information to supply in form elements. Label all form fields with self-explanatory labels, and use the LABEL FOR tag to make explicit associations between form elements and their labels.

9.2.2 Associate related form fields
Form elements are often divided into sections based on the type of information that is being requested, such as contact or shipping information. Use the FIELDSET and LEGEND tags to explicitly associate related form elements.

9.2.3 Design forms for keyboard accessibility
Some users navigate and complete forms using the keyboard. Make all form elements operable from the keyboard, and ensure that their behavior is consistent with user expectations.

9.2.4 Apply a logical sequence to form elements

Keyboard users access Web form elements in the sequence that they appear in the code. Ensure that form elements follow a logical sequence when accessed via the keyboard, and that all essential elements precede the control that submits the form.

9.2.5 Don't auto-populate form fields with text

Using default text to label text input fields creates usability problems for visual and nonvisual users. Use a label rather than default content to indicate the purpose of a text input field.

9.2.6 Use form elements correctly

When used properly, menu fields, such as checkboxes, radio buttons, and select menus, can enhance usability and facilitate data collection. Choose the appropriate menu type, and make item selection an explicit user choice.

Links

10.1 BASIC PRINCIPLES

10.1.1 Use text for links

Access to links is essential for Web usability. Use text for links, and style them using style sheets.

10.1.2 Use descriptive link text

Descriptive link text makes navigation easier and more efficient because descriptive links are easier to skim and allow users to make informed choices. Make link text clear and self-explanatory to support quick and effective navigation.

10.2 Markup

10.2.1 Underline links that are not otherwise identifiable as links

Some users cannot distinguish colors and rely on other visual cues to identify links. Do not rely on color alone to identify links; use underlines or other visual indicators—such as borders or buttons—to mark links.

10.2.2 Differentiate visited and unvisited links

The ability to distinguish between visited and unvisited links helps keep users from revisiting pages that did not prove successful. Differentiate unvisited and visited links so that users can identify the pages that they have already visited.

10.2.3 Provide "you are here" orientation cues

Users can easily become disoriented when navigating the Web. Use orientation cues—such as an arrow marker next to the current page link—to identify the current page.

10.2.4 Use alt-text for image links

Without alt-text, image-based navigation is virtually inaccessible to non-visual users. Provide descriptive alternate text for image links, including links in image maps, for users who cannot access images.

Color

11.1 BASIC PRINCIPLES

11.1.1 Select contrasting colors for greatest legibility

Readability suffers when there is insufficient contrast between text and background. Maximize legibility by using color combinations that contrast in brightness (such as black and white) and hue (such as purple and yellow).

11.1.2 Don't use color alone to convey meaning

Some users cannot see color, while others have difficulties distinguishing certain colors. When using color to convey information, reinforce color with text so people who cannot access color can access the information.

11.2 MARKUP

11.2.1 Allow users to override color settings

Users may need to apply customized color settings to access Web content. Use styles to define colors so users can easily override color settings. Avoid using images, which cannot be customized, for essential page content.

Audio and Video

12.1 BASIC PRINCIPLES

12.1.1 Provide text for audio content

Some users cannot access audio. Supply a text transcript of audio content; when audio is part of video, also synchronize the transcript as captions.

12.1.2 Provide descriptions for video content

Some users cannot access video. Use synchronized descriptions to provide pertinent details about video, along with a separate file containing text descriptions and the audio transcript for users who cannot access video files.

12.1.3 Provide alternate formats for media-based content

Many factors can impede access to media, including physical or technical limitations. When providing content using audio and video, supply alternatives so users can choose the version that best suits their needs and preferences.

12.1.4 Make media keyboard accessible

Some users navigate the Web using the keyboard. Make sure media controls—such as play and pause—respond to keyboard commands, so users who rely on keyboard navigation can control media playback.

12.1.5 Allow users to control media playback

Users should decide when to access media. Make loading and playback of media an explicit user choice, and provide controls for playing, pausing, and controlling volume.

Interactivity

13.1 BASIC PRINCIPLES

13.1.1 Use add-ons for interactivity only when necessary

Add-on technologies—such as JavaScript and Flash—are not as flexible or as accessible as HTML. Explore standard methods fully before resorting to a nonstandard format.

13.1.2 Allow users to control the user interface

Users become disoriented when the interface behaves in ways that are inconsistent with expectations. Do not assume control of elements of the interface that belong in the domain of the user, such as window size and cursor position.

13.1.3 Make interactivity keyboard-accessible

Some users activate elements using the keyboard and will be unable to use an interface that requires point-and-click interaction. Make sure all interactive elements are usable from the keyboard and behave in a manner that is consistent with user expectations.

13.2 MARKUP

13.2.1 Provide an accessible alternate when using a nonstandard format

Some users cannot access interactivity designed using JavaScript or Flash. When providing content in a nonstandard format, provide the equivalent content as accessible HTML.

Editorial Style

14.1 BASIC PRINCIPLES

14.1.1 Break up text into segments

Web readers skim text to form an overview or to locate specific information. Break content into easy-to-skim segments, and use headings to identify the subject of each segment.

14.1.2 Start sentences, headings, and links with keywords

Skimming is more efficient when editorial landmarks begin with keywords. Put important words or phrases at the beginning of sentences, headings, and links.

14.1.3 Adopt a writing style that is clear and to the point

Web readers are goal-oriented and get bogged down by lengthy and unnecessary explanations and instructions. Be concise and factual; avoid meaningless prose.

14.1.4 Use appropriate language and terminology

Users benefit from a writing style that is geared for their knowledge level. Adopt an appropriate writing style and vocabulary, and apply it consistently.

14.1.5 Keep content current and links functional

Out-of-date content and broken links put into question the overall reliability of a site. Revisit content on a regular basis to validate and repair links and to update or remove content.

14.2 MARKUP

14.2.1 Mark up language changes within a document

Software can read documents more accurately when language changes are identified. Indicate the primary document language, and use markup to mark language changes.

14.2.2 Identify and describe abbreviations and acronyms

Software can provide clarifying information for abbreviations and acronyms. For improved screen reader access, use style sheets to indicate whether these elements should be spoken or spelled out.

14.2.3 Provide a print option for lengthy documents

Some people prefer to print longer documents for offline reading. Provide a single-page printing version for documents that are likely to be printed.

Page Layout

15.1 BASIC PRINCIPLES

15.1.1 Design pages for linear access

Software reads the code of Web pages from top to bottom. Make sure the sequence of content is logical in the code. Put important content first, and group related content.

15.1.2 Communicate visual information to nonvisual users

Some users cannot access information communicated via visual design. Make sure all relevant information that is communicated visually—through indents, spacing, proximity, and so on—is also conveyed in the code.

15.1.3 Apply a consistent design

Users must learn how to use the Web at each site, and often within a single site, as the design and functional elements change from page to page. Adopt design conventions and a consistent navigation scheme for improved usability.

15.1.4 Balance content and navigation

Many links make for busy, overwhelming pages. Rather than overload pages with navigation options, focus on presenting content and context-sensitive navigation.

15.1.5 Provide navigation tools

Users often have difficulty finding what they are seeking. Provide tools to help users locate content, such as search, site index, site map, and quick links.

15.2 MARKUP

15.2.1 Design flexible page layouts

Users who enlarge type or view pages on a small display need a flexible layout that will adapt to their viewing environment. Design flexible layouts using relative measurements.

15.2.2 Use style sheets for layout whenever possible

Flexibility is best achieved when content and presentation are separate. Design pages using structural markup, and use style sheets to control page layout.

15.2.3 Provide direct access to page content

Pages that begin with nonessential content can prove cumbersome for some users. Place content close to the top of each page, marked by a heading. Alternatively, provide a visible "Skip to main content" link at the beginning of each page.

References

GENERAL DESIGN

Bringhurst, Robert. *The Elements of Typographic Style,* 2nd ed. Vancouver: Hartley and Marks, 2004.

Kufmann Jr., Edgar. *What Is Modern Design?* New York: The Museum of Modern Art, 1950.

Lidwell, William, Kristina Holden, and Jill Butler. *Universal Principles of Design.* Gloucester, MA: Rockport Publishers, 2003.

Marcus, George H. *What Is Design Today?* New York: Abrams, 2002.

Pile, John F. *Design.* Amherst, MA: The University of Massachusetts Press, 1979.

Rehe, Rolf F. *Typography: How To Make It Most Legible.* Carmel, IN: Design Research International, 1974.

Rogers, Everett M. *The Diffusion of Innovations,* 4th ed. New York: The Free Press, 1995.

Sullivan, Louis H. "The Tall Office Building Artistically Considered." *Lippincott's Magazine,* March 1896. Available online at http://www.njit.edu/old/Library/archlib/pub-domain/sullivan-1896-tall-bldg.html.

Tinker, Miles. *Legibility of Print.* Ames, IA: Iowa State University Press, 1963.

Tufte, Edward. *Envisioning Information.* Cheshire, CT: Graphics Press, 1990.

Wheildon, Colin. *Type & Layout: How Typography and Design Can Get Your Message Across, or Get in the Way.* Berkeley: Strathmoor Press, 1996.

Williams, Robin. *The Nondesigner's Design Book.* Berkeley: Peachpit Press, 1994.

UNIVERSAL DESIGN

Connell, Bettye Rose, Mike Jones, Ron Mace, Jim Mueller, Abir Mullick, Elaine Ostroff, Jon Sanford, Ed Steinfeld, Molly Story, and Gregg Vanderheiden. "Principles of Universal Design." North Carolina State University, The Center for Universal Design, 1997. http://www.design.ncsu.edu/cud/univ_design/princ_overview.htm.

Dreyfuss, Henry. *Designing for People.* New York: Allworth Press, 2003. First published 1955 by Simon and Schuster.

Henry Dreyfuss Associates. *The Measure of Man and Woman: Human Factors in Design.* New York: Whitney Library of Design, 1993. First published 1959 under the title: *The Measure of Man.*

Story, Molly Follette. *The Universal Design File: Designing for People of All Ages and Abilities.* Raleigh, NC: North Carolina State University, Center for Universal Design, 1998.

Preiser, Wolfgang, and Elaine Ostroff, eds. *Universal Design Handbook.* New York: McGraw-Hill Professional, 2001.

Trace Research and Development Center. "General Concepts, Universal Design Principles and Guidelines." http://trace.wisc.edu/world/gen_ud.html.

INTERFACE DESIGN

Association for Computing Machinery (ACM). Special Interest Group on Computer-Human Interaction (SIGCHI). http://www.acm.org/sigchi/.

———. Special Interest Group on Accessible Computing (SIGACCESS). http://www.hcibib.org/accessibility/.

———. Conference on Universal Usability. http://www.sigchi.org/cuu/.

IBM Corporation. *IBM Ease of Use.* http://www-306.ibm.com/ibm/easy/eou_ext.nsf/publish/558.

Mullet, K., and Darrell Sano. *Designing Visual Interfaces: Communications-Oriented Techniques.* Mountain View, CA: SunSoft Press, 1995.

Norman, Donald. *The Design of Everyday Things.* New York: Basic Books, 2002.

Norman, Donald. *The Invisible Computer: Why Good Products Can Fail, the Personal Computer Is So Complex, and Information Appliances Are the Solution.* Cambridge, MA: MIT Press, 1999.

Shneiderman, Ben. *Leonardo's Laptop: Human Needs and the New Computing Technologies.* Cambridge, MA: MIT Press, 2003.

Shneiderman, Ben. "Universal Usability." *Communications of the ACM* 43, no. 5 (May 2000): 84–91.

Shneiderman, Ben and Catherine Plaisant. *Designing the User Interface: Strategies for Effective Human-Computer Interaction*, 4th ed. Boston: Addison Wesley Professional, 2004.

WEB DESIGN

A list apart. http://www.alistapart.com/.

Agelight. "Interface Design Guidelines for Users of All Ages." Agelight LLC, 2001. http://www.agelight.com/Resources/webdesign.htm.

Berners-Lee, Tim. *Weaving the Web: The Original Design and Ultimate Destiny of the World Wide Web by Its Inventor.* New York: HarperCollins, 2000.

Boxes and Arrows: The Design Behind the Design. http://boxesandarrows.com/.

Cederholm, Dan. *Web Standards Solutions: The Markup and Style Handbook.* Berkeley: Friends of ED, 2004.

Cockburn, Andy, Saul Greenberg, Steve Jones, Bruce Mckenzie, and Michael Moyle. "Improving Web Page Revisitation: Analysis, Design, and Evaluation." *IT & Society* 1, no. 3 (Winter 2003): 159–183.

CSS Zen Garden: The Beauty in CSS Design. http://www.csszengarden.com/.

Digital Web Magazine. http://www.digital-web.com/.

Hill, Alyson, and Lauren Scharff. "Readability of Web Sites with Various Foreground/Background Color Combinations, Font Types, and Word Styles." 1997. http://hubel.sfasu.edu/research/AHNCUR.html.

Horton, Sarah. "Forging a Partnership Between Designer and User." *Digital Web Magazine*, September 1, 2004. http://digital-web.com/articles/designer_user_partnership/.

Horton, Sarah. "Beauty Is Only Screen Deep." *Boxes and Arrows,* October 14, 2002. http://www.boxesandarrows.com/archives/beauty_is_only_screen_deep.php.

Krug, Steve. *Don't Make Me Think: A Common Sense Approach to Web Usability.* Indianapolis: Que, 2001.

Lynch, Patrick, and Sarah Horton. *Web Style Guide: Basic Design Principles for Creating Web Sites,* 2nd ed. New Haven: Yale University Press, 2002. Also available online at http://www.webstyleguide.com/.

Meyer, Eric. *Cascading Style Sheets: The Definitive Guide.* Sebastopol, CA: O'Reilly, 2000.

Meyer, Eric. *Eric Meyer on CSS: Mastering the Language of Web Design.* Indianapolis: New Riders, 2003

Meyer, Eric. "*Really* Undoing HTML.CSS." *Meyerweb.com,* September 15, 2004. http://www.meyerweb.com/eric/thoughts/2004/09/15/emreallyem-undoing-htmlcss/.

Moss, Trenton. "Writing Effective Link Text." *Evolt.org*, July 23, 2004. http://www.evolt.org/article/Writing_effective_link_text/4090/60343/.

Musciano, Chuck and Bill Kennedy. *HTML & XHTML: The Definitive Guide,* 5th ed. Sebastopol, CA: O'Reilly, 2002.

Nielsen, Jakob. *Designing Web Usability: The Practice of Simplicity.* Indianapolis: New Riders, 2000.

Nielsen, Jakob. *The Alertbox: Current ssues in Web Usability.* http://www.useit.com/alertbox/.

Nielsen, Jakob. "How Users Read on the Web." *The Alertbox: Current Issues in Web Usability,* October 1, 1997. http://www.useit.com/alertbox/9710a.html.

Nielsen, Jakob, and Marie Tahir. *Homepage Usability: 50 Web Sites Deconstructed.* Indianapolis: New Riders, 2002.

Shea, Dave, and Molly E. Holzschlag. *The Zen of css Design*. Berkeley: Peachpit Press, 2005.

Koyani, Sanjay J., Robert W. Bailey, Janice R. Nall, Conrad Mulligan, Susan Allison, Kent Bailey, and Mark Tolson. *Research-Based Web Design and Usability Guidelines*. U.S. Department of Health and Human Services, September 2003. http://usability.gov/pdfs/guidelines.html.

Usability News. http://psychology.wichita.edu/surl/usability_news.html.

Veen, Jeffrey. *The Art and Science of Web Design*. Indianapolis: New Riders, 2000.

Zeldman. Jeffrey. *Designing with Web Standards*. Indianapolis: New Riders, 2003.

WEB ACCESSIBILITY

Adobe. *Adobe: Accessibility*. http://www.adobe.com/enterprise/accessibility/.

Arditi, Aries. "Effective Color Contrast: Designing for People with Partial Sight and Color Deficiencies." Lighthouse International, 2005. http://www.lighthouse.org/color_contrast.htm.

Arditi, Aries. "Making Text Legible: Designing for People with Partial Sight." Lighthouse International, 2005. http://www.lighthouse.org/print_leg.htm.

Brewer, Judy, ed. "How People with Disabilities Use the Web." w3c, 2004. http://www.w3.org/WAI/EO/Drafts/PWD-Use-Web/.

Chisholm, Wendy, Gregg Vanderheiden, and Ian Jacobs, eds. "Web Content Accessibility Guidelines 1.0." w3c, 1999. http://www.w3.org/TR/WAI-WEBCONTENT/.

Chong, Curtis. "Making Your Web Site Accessible to the Blind." National Federation of the Blind, 2002. http://www.nfb.org/tech/webacc.htm.

Clark, Joe. *Building Accessible Web Sites*. Indianapolis: New Riders, 2003.

CPB/WGBH National Center for Accessible Media. *Rich Media Resource Center*. http://ncam.wgbh.org/richmedia/.

Freedom Scientific. "The HTML Challenge." 2003. http://www. freedomscientific.com/HTML_challenge/.

Horton, Sarah. "Making Web Accessible to All." *New York Times*, June 10, 2002, c4. Also available online at http://www.nytimes.com/ 2002/06/10/technology/10NECO.html.

IBM Corporation. "Web Accessibility Developer Guidelines." 2004. http://www-3.ibm.com/able/guidelines/web/accessweb.html.

Macromedia. *Accessibility Resource Center*. http://www.macromedia. com/resources/accessibility/.

Paciello, Michael G. *Web Accessibility for People with Disabilities*. Gilroy, CA: CMP Books, 2000.

Pilgrim, Mark. *Dive into Accessibility*, 2002. http://diveintoaccessibility. org/.

Regan, Bob. "Best Practices for Accessible Flash Design." *Bob Regan: Accessibility,* May 2004. http://www.markme.com/accessibility/files/ Best%20Practices%20for%20Accessible%20Flash%20Design.pdf.

Slatin, John M., and Sharron Rush. *Maximum Accessibility: Making Your Web Site More Usable for Everyone*. Boston: Addison Wesley Professional, 2002.

Thatcher, Jim, Paul Bohman, Michael Burks, Shawn Lawton Henry, Bob Regan, Sarah Swierenga, Mark D. Urban, and Cynthia D. Waddell. *Constructing Accessible Web sites*. Birmingham, UK: glasshaus, 2002.

WebAIM: Web Accessibility in Mind. http://www.webaim.org/.

Illustration Credits

INTRODUCTION

1 Smith & Hawken. www.smithandhawken.com. © 2005 Smith & Hawken, Ltd. All rights reserved. Used courtesy of Smith & Hawken.

2 Amazon. www.amazon.com. © 2005 Amazon.com, Inc. All rights reserved.

3 National Park Service - Hawaii Volcanoes National Park. www.nps.gov. In the public domain.

4 Microsoft Accessibility. www.microsoft.com. © 2005 Microsoft Corporation. All rights reserved. Microsoft product screen shot reprinted with permission from Microsoft Corporation.

5 ESPN. espn.go.com. © 2005 ESPN Internet Ventures. All rights reserved.

6 HubbleSite. www.hubblesite.org. In the public domain.

7 *Wired News*. www.wired.com. © 2005 Lycos, Inc. All rights reserved. Reprinted from Wired News.

8 Google. www.google.com. © 2005 Google. Google and the Google logo are trademarks of Google Technology, Inc.

FUNDAMENTALS

1.1 Netflix. www.netflix.com. © 1997–2005 Netflix, Inc.

1.2 *Wired News. See* 7.

1.3 TigerDirect.com. www.tigerdirect.com. © 2005 TigerDirect, Inc.

1.4 Network for Good. www.networkforgood.org. © 2005 Network for Good. All rights reserved.

1.5 LEGO.com. www.lego.com. © 2005 The LEGO Group. LEGO and the LEGO logo are trademarks of the LEGO Group, here used with special permission.

1.6 U.S. Copyright Office. www.copyright.gov. In the public domain.

1.7 OXO International. www.oxo.com. © 2004 OXO International, Ltd.

1.8 Anywho. www.anywho.com. © 2005 AT&T Corp. All rights reserved. Reprinted with permission, AT&T Corp.

1.9 KidsHealth. www.kidshealth.org. Courtesy of KidsHealth.org/ The Nemours Foundation © 2004.

1.10 W3Schools. www.w3schools.com. © 1999–2005 by Refsnes Data. All rights reserved.

1.11 IBM Ease of Use. www.ibm.com. Reprint courtesy of International Business Machines Corporation © International Business Machines Corporation.

1.12 *Fast Company.* www.fastcompany.com. © 2005 Grunar + Jahr USA Publishing. First published in Fastcompany.com. Reprinted with permission.

DOCUMENT STRUCTURE

2.1 Wikipedia. www.wikipedia.org. Licensed under the GNU Free Documentation License, www.gnu.org/copyleft/fdl.html.

2.2 Wikipedia. *See* 2.1.

2.3 *Boxes and Arrows.* www.boxesandarrows.com. © 2002–2005 Boxes and Arrows.

2.5 CSS Zen Garden. www.csszengarden.com. © 2001–2005 Dave Shea. All rights reserved.

2.6 *BBC News.* news.bbc.co.uk. © BBC. From BBC News at bbcnews.co.uk.

TEXT

3.1 Audible. www.audible.com. © 1997–2005 Audible, Inc.

3.2 Blogger. www.blogger.com. © 1999–2005 Google Inc. Blogger and the "B" design are trademarks of Google Inc.

3.3 U.S. Department of Education. www.ed.gov. In the pubic domain. MedlinePlus. www.medlineplus.gov. In the public domain.

3.4 *The Atlantic Online*. www.theatlantic.com. © 2005 by The Atlantic Monthly Group. Design by Eric Westby.

3.5 *Wall Street Journal*. online.wsj.com. © 2005 Dow Jones & Company, Inc. All rights reserved.

3.6 Solar System Exploration. solarsystem.nasa.gov. In the public domain.

3.7 Network for Good. *See* 1.4.

3.8 *A List Apart*. www.alistapart.com. © 1998–2005 A List Apart Magazine and Happy Cog Studios.

IMAGES

4.1 Shopzilla. www.shopzilla.com. © 2005 Shopzilla, Inc.

4.2 Microsoft. *See* 4.

4.3 Surprise.com. www.surprise.com. © 2005 Surprise.com, Inc. All rights reserved.

4.4 Network for Good. *See* 1.4.

4.5 About.com. www.about.com. © 2005 About, Inc. All rights reserved. Used with permission of About, Inc.

4.6 Nutrition.gov. www.nutrition.gov. In the pubic domain.

4.7 NextD. www.nextd.org. © 2005 NextDesign Leadership Institute: New York. All rights reserved.

4.8 NASA. www.nasa.gov. Used with permission.

4.9 Creative Commons. www.creativecommons.org. Provided under the terms of a Creative Commons license.

4.10 Daffodils. © Paul Horton 2005. www.paulhortonphoto.com.

4.11 Foureye Butterflyfish, *Chaetodon capistratus*. © 2005 Patrick Lynch. www.patricklynch.net.

4.12 *National Geographic Magazine.* www.nationalgeographic.com. Courtesy © 2004 The National Geographic Society. All rights reserved. Photos © 2005 Frans Lanting. www.lanting.com.

DATA TABLES

5.1 Bronx Zoo. www.bronxzoo.com. © 1998–2003 Wildlife Conservation Society. All rights reserved.

5.2 National Pubic Radio (NPR). www.npr.org. © 2005 NPR. Courtesy of NPR®.

5.3 W3Schools. *See* 1.10.

5.4 American Factfinder. www.factfinder.census.gov. In the public domain.

LAYOUT TABLES

6.1 IBM Education. *See* 1.11.

6.2 Amazon. www.amazon.com. © 2005 Amazon.com, Inc. All rights reserved. eBay. www.eBay.com. © 1995-2005 eBay, Inc. All rights reserved. CNN. www.cnn.com. © 2005 Cable News Network. All rights reserved. *The Atlantic Online. See* 3.4.

6.3 *Wired News. See* 7.

6.4 Lonely Planet. www.lonelyplanet.com. Reproduced with permission from the Lonely Planet website © Lonely Planet Publications. Images from www.lonelyplanetimages.com.

6.5 National Air & Space Museum - The Wright Brothers. www.nasm.si.edu/wrightbrothers. Smithsonian, National Air and Space Museum.

6.6 National Park Service. *See* 3.

6.7 *The Chronicle of Higher Education.* www.chronicle.com. © 2004 The Chronicle of Higher Education. Reprinted with permission.

6.8 Microsoft Windows - Internet Explorer. *See* 4.

FRAMES

7.1 *NextD Journal. See* 4.7.

7.2 ComputerUser.com - High-tech Dictionary. www. computeruser.com/resources/dictionary. © 2005 Key Professional Media, Inc.

LISTS

8.1 Salon. www.salon.com. © 2005 Salon Media Group. All rights reserved. The "S" logo is a licensed trademark of Salon Media Group.

8.2 Motley Fool. www.fool.com. © 1995–2005 The Motley Fool, Inc. All rights reserved.

FORMS

9.1 MapQuest. www.mapquest.com. © 2005 MapQuest.com, Inc. All rights reserved.

9.2 Peet's Coffee and Tea. www.peets.com. © 2004–2005 Peet's Coffee and Tea.

9.3 Infospace. www.infospace.com. © 1998–2005 InfoSpace, Inc. All rights reserved.

9.4 My Yahoo! my.yahoo.com. Reproduced with permission of Yahoo! Inc. © 2005 by Yahoo! Inc. YAHOO! And the YAHOO! logo are trademarks of Yahoo! Inc.

9.5 Adobe. www.adobe.com. © 2005 Adobe Systems Incorporated. All rights reserved. Adobe, Adobe Studio, GoLive and Illustrator are registered trademarks of Adobe Systems Incorporated in the United States and other countries

9.6 Amazon. *See* 6.2.

9.7 MedlinePlus. *See* 3.3. National Park Service. *See* 3. National Library of Medicine. www.nlm.nih.gov. In the public domain.

9.8 IBM Contact. *See* 1.11.

LINKS

10.1 KidsHealth. *See* 1.9.

10.2 Wikipedia. *See* 2.1.

10.3 Audible. *See* 3.1.

10.4 Westciv. www.westciv.com. © 1997–2005 Western Civilisation Pty Ltd.

10.5 Shutterfly. www.shutterfly.com. © Shutterfly 1999–2005. All rights reserved.

10.6 HubbleSite. *See* 6.

10.7 IBM Accessibility Center. *See* 1.11.

10.8 Nutrition.gov. *See* 4.6.

10.9 *Digital Web Magazine.* www.digital-web.com. © 1994–2005 Digital Web Magazine. All rights reserved.

10.10 Epinions. www.epinions.com. © 1999–2005 Epinions, Inc.

COLOR

11.1 YellowstonePark.com. www.yellowstonepark.com. © 2005 Yellowstone Journal Corporation. Photography by Jeff Vanuga and Jeff Henry. The Colour Contrast Analyser was developed by Jun of Wrong HTML (html.idena.jp) in collaboration with Steve Faulkner from Accessible Information Solutions (www.nils.org.au/ais).

11.3 Tribeworks. www.tribeworks.com. © 2005 Tribeworks, Inc. All rights reserved.

11.4 UNICEF. www.unicefusa.org. United States Fund for UNICEF. All rights reserved. Screenshot courtesy of the U.S. Fund for UNICEF, 1-800-4-UNICEF.

11.5 Simple Bits. www.simplebits.com. © 1999–2005 SimpleBits. All rights reserved.

AUDIO AND VIDEO

12.1 White House Speeches. www.whitehouse.gov. In the public domain.

12.2 NOVA - scienceNOW. www.pbs.org/wgbh/nova/sciencenow. © 2005 WGBH Educational Foundation. All rights reserved.

12.3 Dignubia. www.dignubia.org. © 2005 Education Development Center, Inc. All rights reserved.

12.4 National Geographic - Forces of Nature. *See* 4.12.

12.5 Fourth Annual Media that Matters Film Festival. www.mediathatmattersfest.org/mtm04. Courtesy of Arts Engine, Inc.

12.6 P.O.V. www.pbs.org/pov. Courtesy of P.O.V. Interactive © 1995-2004 American Documentary, Inc.

INTERACTIVITY

13.1 Iberia. www.iberia.com. © 2005 Iberia. All rights reserved.

13.2 Expedia. www.expedia.com. © 2005 Expedia, Inc. All rights reserved.

13.3 Meetup. www.meetup.com. © 2002–2005 Meetup Inc. Provided by Meetup.com.

13.4 John F. Kennedy International Airport. www.panynj.gov/aviation/jfkframe.htm. Courtesy of Port Authority of NY & NJ.

13.5 NCES Students' Classroom. nces.ed.gov/nceskids. National Center for Education Statistics, U.S. Department of Education. In the public domain.

13.6 NOVA -Infinite Secrets. www.pbs.org/wgbh/nova/archimedes. © 2005 WGBH Educational Foundation. All rights reserved.

EDITORIAL STYLE

14.1 IBM Ease of Use. *See* 1.11.

14.2 Wikipedia. *See* 2.1.

14.3 National Library of Medicine. *See* 9.7.

14.4 evolt.org. www.evolt.org. Used with permission.

14.5 InformIT. www.informit.com. © 2005 Pearson Education, Informit. All rights reserved. Courtesy of www.informit.com.

PAGE LAYOUT

15.1 Motley Fool. *See 8.2.*

15.2 *Boxes and Arrows. See 2.3. Web Style Guide.* www.webstyleguide. com. © 2002 Lynch and Horton. *A List Apart. See 3.8.*

15.3 National Air & Space Museum - The Wright Brothers. *See 6.5.*

15.4 Meetup. *See 13.3.*

15.5 Shutterfly. *See 10.5.*

15.6 The Museum of Modern Art. www.moma.org. © 2005 The Museum of Modern Art.

15.7 Informit. *See 14.5.*

15.8 Mayo Clinic. www.mayoclinic.com. © Mayo Foundation for Medical Education and Research. All rights reserved. Used with permission from www.MayoClinic.com.

15.9 Centers for Disease Control and Prevention. www.cdc.gov. In the public domain. National Library of Medicine. *See 9.7.*

15.10 CNET. www.cnet.com. © 1995-2005 CNET Networks, Inc. All rights reserved.

15.11 *Fast Company. See 1.12.*

15.12 Blogger. *See 3.2.*

Index

Bringhurst, Robert *xvi,* 23
Bronx Zoo site 90
browsers
    and CSS 44, 50, 100–101
    and frames-based pages 111
    and graphic text 75
    how text is displayed by 6
    and layout tables 97
    and text size 39
    for visual *vs.* nonvisual users 3
bulleted lists 184

cameras *ix*
CAPTION tag 94–95, 97
captions 62, 80–81, 94–95, 164, 165
Cascading Style Sheets. *See* CSS
cataloging images 83
CDC site 207
Census Bureau site 94
checkboxes 137, 138
Chicago Manual of Style 201
Chronicle of Higher Education site 107
citations 48–49
CNET site 209
color 155–161
    allowing users to override 160–161
    background 64–65
    basic principles regarding 155–160
    contrast considerations 64–65,
        155–157
    conveying information with
        66–67, 158–160
    as design tool 155
    for links 147, 149
    and nonvisual users 66–67, 155,
        158–160
    reinforcing with text 159–160
    for text 64–67, 157, 159–160
    unpredictability of 37
    using style sheets to set 65–66
    and visual users 155, 158–160

Color Contrast Analyzer software 156
column headings, table 93–94
communication function, Web page
    4–5
compound lists 122–123
compression schemes 85
Computer User High-Tech Dictionary
    site 116
Conference on Universal Usability *xi*
conferences, Web design *xi*
content
    allowing quick access to 214
    audio (*See* audio content)
    balancing navigation and 203–205
    encoding with structural tags 49,
        67–69
    grouping related 197
    keeping fresh/current 188–189
    positioning important 213–215
    providing universal access to
        44–45
    separating presentation and
        43, 44–47
    video (*See* video content)
content layer, Web design *xx*
contrast, color 64–65, 155–157
conventions, design 201–203
Copyright site 32
Creative Commons site 82
CSS. *See also* style sheets
    assigning cell widths with 108
    benefits of 50–52
    browser support for 44, 50,
        100–101
    meaning of acronym 44
    and navigation design 121
    as page layout tool 100–101
    styling text with 59
    vs. HTML 46–47
    ways of using 46–47
CSS Zen Garden site 50, 51

marking language changes 189
providing keywords 185–186
providing print option 191
using appropriate language/
terminology 187
Elements of Style, The 186
Elements of Typographical Design, The
23
embedded media content 170
embedded styles 54–55, 59
emphasized words 49
Envisioning Information 26
Epinions site 153
ESPN 15
Evolt.org site 190
Expedia site 175
external style sheets 59

fallbacks 23, 28
Fast Company site 40, 212
FIELDSET tag 131
fixed design 14–18, 25
fixed layouts 12, 63, 106–107
Flash 30, 133, 173, 175, 180
flexibility, Web page 8–9, 11–14, 25
flexible design 17, 18–21, 25
flexible layouts 11–14, 64, 106–108,
208–211
FONT tag 43, 48, 49
footnotes 62
form design 125–129
form fields. *See also* forms
associating related 131
auto-populating fields in 135–137
labeling 126, 129–131, 137
"form follows function" formula 1–2
forms 126–139
applying logical sequence to
elements in 134
associating related fields in 125, 131
auto-populating fields in 135–137

avoiding redundancy in 128
basic principles regarding 126–129
designing 125–128
grouping related elements in 125,
127
labeling fields in 126, 129–131, 137
and nonvisual users 130, 134
providing alternate to 126, 128–129
providing keyboard access to
132–134
purpose of 125
using menu-style elements in
137–139
frame titles 114–115
frames 111–117
avoiding use of 112–114
and back button 112
basic principles regarding 112–114
and bookmarking 111, 112
browser considerations 111
defined 111
identifying functions of 114–115
and nonvisual users 111–112, 113,
114–115
printing considerations 111, 112
pros and cons of 111–112
providing alternative to 115–117
FRAMESET tag 114
framesets 112
function
defining 2–5
form *vs.*, 1–2, 10
providing 10–21
functional layer, Web design *xix–xx*

GIF images 85
global navigation 204
Google site 20
graphic design *xvi*, 14
graphic text 58–59, 75–76

Designed and typeset by Sarah Horton
Cover design by Mimi Heft
Printed by Courier

The text face is Adobe Caslon Pro, designed by Carol Twombly, based on designs by 18th century type founder William Caslon.

Editorial landmarks, such as headings, labels, and callouts, are set in Syntax, designed by Hans Eduard Meyer for the Stempel foundry.

Code examples are set using a monospaced font, Andale Mono, created by Steve Matteson for the Monotype Corporation.

The oak tree symbol, part of the Greymantle font, designed by Kanna Aoki and digitized by Mark van Bronkhorst, is used as a reminder of the dictum "form follows function," as symbolized by "the branching oak" in Louis H. Sullivan's essay (see Introduction, page 1), and as a personal reminder of the abiding spirit of my brother.